Batsford Book of CANVAS WORK

In needle works there doth great knowledg rest.
A fine conceit thereby full soone is showne:
A drowsie braine this skill cannot digest,
Paine spent on such, in vaine awaie is throne;
They must be carefull, diligent and wise,
In needleworkes that beare away the prise.

Then prettie maidens view this prettie booke,
Marke well the works that you therein doe finde:
Sitting at worke cast not aside your looke,
They profit small that have a gazing minde.
Keep cleane your Samplers, sleepe not as you sit:
For sluggishness doth spoile the rarest wit.

Anon
(Published by Willm Barley, London, 1596)

Jacket illustrations:
Abstract Panel, designed and worked by the author for the River Valley Chapter of the Embroiderers' Guild of America in Connecticut, 1981. This panel is worked on white, 14-mesh, interlocked canvas with Appleton wools, coton à broder, silk and Twilley's gold and black gold-fingering thread. The stitches used include fan-tail, fan vaulting, arrow half-drop filling, spring, diagonal broad cross, expanding wheatsheaf and Rhodes

Batsford Book of CANVAS WORK

MARY RHODES

B T BATSFORD LTD LONDON

ISBN 0 7134 2669 1

Typeset by Tek-Art Ltd, London
and printed in Great Britain by
The Anchor Press Ltd
Tiptree, Essex
for the publishers
B T Batsford Ltd
4 Fitzhardinge Street
London W1H 0AH

Contents

Acknowledgment

I should like to thank the numerous people, who have assisted me in various ways in the preparation of material for composing this book. First of all I must thank Miss Thelma King, Librarian at Westminster Library, London, for her invaluable help in obtaining many important books for me to consult on various aspects of the subject over the years. I should also like to thank members of the staff at the Bible Society and the Guildhall in London, together with Mrs Young at the British Museum and members of the photographic departments, both at the British Museum and at the Victoria and Albert Museum, for their assistance in obtaining the necessary photographs of early pieces of canvas work. In addition I express my thanks to the many friends, who have helped me by kindly lending me examples of their work to photograph, and to Mrs Patricia Anderson of Long Beach, California, USA for her kindness in giving me permission to include a photograph of her eighteenth century piece of canvas work, showing St Cecilia at the organ. I should also like to thank Mrs Grace Abbott of Aberdeen, New Jersey, USA for introducing me to the Four-needle Norwich Stitch. My greatest debt of gratitude, however, goes to my husband Val, who has photographed all except the historical pieces, typed the manuscript, helped with checking the proofs of the book and, needless to say, given me assistance in a hundred and one other ways, too numerous to mention.

Eltham, London, 1982   M.R.

Unless otherwise stated, all the modern pieces of canvas work are designed by Mary Rhodes.

Introduction

The type of embroidery I am attempting to describe in this book has been given a variety of names both here and in other parts of the world: it is called canvas embroidery, petit-point, canvas needlework, tapestry work and needlepoint, in addition to canvas work, which is the name most commonly used to describe it in this country today and the one I have chosen for the title of this book.

Very little now remains of the canvas work of the early years of our history, and in my attempt to trace its development through the ages, it has not always been easy to differentiate between what was definitely canvas work and what was some other form of embroidery of the time. I have, therefore, been obliged to identify this early canvas work by the stitches used, such as tent stitch, plaited stitch and cross stitch, and, on certain rare occasions, two-sided Italian stitch and eyelets. I have included some pieces of work from the period of the *Opus Anglicanum*, which have backgrounds of gold, worked in straight stitch (Gobelin) in geometric stitch patterns, which would necessitate the use of an even-weave fabric.

Only a very few pieces of early work now remain for us to observe out of the enormous amount, which, according to written records, was originally produced. Various events, together with the constantly changing conditions of life over the years, which included hundreds of years of general wear and tear, devasting fires, damp, moth and other insect damage, theft and wanton destruction, as well as changes of fashion, have all contributed to the loss of much of the finery of early days, and the real wonder is that we now have left as much as we do. Many of the world's museums, as well as private collections, contain excellent pieces of early work for us to gaze upon and marvel at the luxuriant beauty and extravagance of those days.

History clearly shows how high peaks of production have occurred at various times, and how changes of fashion have from time to time affected craft-work of all kinds. Nobody knows, however, why certain things should have happened exactly when they did, why suddenly in the sixteenth century, for instance, there should have been such an outpouring of canvas work of a high professional standard both in this country and also in France, and why so many ladies in the next century were attracted to that curious art form of raised work (stump work). The nineteenth century, which probably produced more canvas work than any other period in history, not only in Britain, but also in Europe and the United States of America, is more fully documented than other periods, so that we are well aware of the origin of Berlin Wool Work, and why it became such an obsession with the majority of the upper- and middle-class population at that time. In the early years of the twentieth century canvas work declined, until it reached a very low level and, in fact, almost died out altogether, but today it is showing a great improvement, and in the many exhibitions of embroidery, which are held now-a-days, numerous examples of outstandingly good and well-designed modern canvas work may be seen. Canvas work is also enormously popular over the whole of the United States of America, where much splendid work is being produced, and where the designs used follow the same trends as in Britain, with much experimentation, not only in the basic elements of the designs, but also in the use of colour and stitchery.

Canvas work is a fascinating craft, which can supply a life-time of interest, and, although the actual process of working on canvas is slow and time-consuming, the fact that it has appealed to so many people over the ages, and is still today attracting vast numbers the world over, gives hope that its future is secure, and that interest in the craft will continue for many more years to come.

Water-lilies This panel was designed by the author in 1955, and over the succeeding ten years as many as three copies of it were worked in tent stitch on 16 mesh canvas with silk and natural dyed wools. The piece depicted here was the last one of the three to be worked: it is dated 1965 and bears the initials SER

The origin and early history of canvas work

The story of embroidery is a very long one, and its roots go far back into mankind's earliest history. Some form of stitchery can be traced back to the days when early man roamed the earth as a hunter, and the animals he killed provided skins which were used to clothe him and his family. Pieces of skin would require to be stitched together, and for this purpose a fine bone or a strong thorn could have had a hole pierced in it to make a needle which would take a fibre of some kind that could have been obtained from plants, or even from a fine sinew of an animal. In order to join skins together it would probably require something more than simple oversewing, and the use of a second row of stitchery could have led on to the development of cross stitch and a form of herring-bone stitch.

In these same early days the rough intertwining of twigs, rushes and grasses led primitive peoples to the weaving of fibres to make pieces of material, which could also be stitched together to form garments. As time progressed this early stitchery was developed further, until it was used to provide decoration on garments as well as a means of joining pieces of material together. This was the real beginning of the art of embroidery, but no one knows with any certainty when or where it reached the stage of being purely decorative. Most authorities will agree that, as far as this country is concerned — and Europe generally — embroidery as a decorative art emanated from the Middle East, where both weaving and embroidery had already reached a high standard back in pre-classical times. We possess no actual, tangible evidence of this early work, and can only make a conjecture as to its real nature, deriving our information from literary sources. The early woven materials, upon which embroidery could

have been carried out, were probably made from a variety of fibres, such as hemp, jute and flax, and it would have been but a short step to the spinning and plying of hair and wool from various animals. These fibres would then have been woven on primitive frames, and, no doubt, simple back-strap looms were also developed quite early, in using which the warp is tied on to a small branch of a tree, which is itself tied to a post, set in the ground, and the other ends of the warp are tied to another branch of a tree, which is then attached to the weaver, either by means of a strong piece of the warp fibre, or by using a narrow band of material, passed around the lower part of his back. In this way the weaver could control the tension in the work by moving his body backwards or forwards as he was weaving. Such information about early

Early Egyptian Loom   A horizontal loom as depicted in a wall-painting in the tomb of Chnem-hotep at Beni-Hasan, which dates from the period 2000 to 1200 BC. This illustration is from Rosellini's *Monumenti Civili*, Plate XLI

weaving has been obtained by studying the methods and the implements of primitive people in various parts of the world, and from observing tomb paintings in Egypt, such as that in the tomb of Chnem-hotep at Beni Hasan, which shows a horizontal loom, dating from about 2000 to 1200 BC (XII to XIV Dynasties).

Looms like this were probably used to produce a simple tabby-weave material, which could be employed in the making not only of garments but also of a variety of other objects, such as hangings and walls of tents. Linen was used at that time for both warp and weft, and this resulted in the production of a very fine-mesh material upon which it was possible to carry out excellent examples of embroidery. This work was performed in various parts of the Middle East, but notably in Egypt, Syria, Persia, and Byzantium.

We know that textile art was also understood in early days in Far Eastern countries, especially in India and China, and that silken fabrics were produced in China as early as 3000 BC. Later, in about 1200 BC, when the Chinese Empire was subdivided into many feudal states, the members of individual states rivalled each other in the luxury of their dress and surrounded themselves with artists skilled in weaving and embroidery. We cannot, however, be sure whether or not it was in that part of the world that the art of embroidery originated, spreading on from there later to the Middle East and Europe. The widespread conquests of Alexander the Great, which brought the Greeks into contact not only with Egypt and Persia but also with India, may have led to the intake of fresh ideas on embroidery from India into the western world. We know that Alexander succumbed to all the refinements of Asiatic luxury, and that his common tent was lined with woven tapestries and embroideries worked in gold. What is clear is that we in Europe owe our present knowledge of embroidery to what was done in the Middle East many years previously.

The early tabby-weave material, we have already mentioned as the probable basis upon which embroidery came to be worked, was the forerunner of our present-day canvas used in doing modern canvas work. Over the years, however, the actual nature of this basic canvas material has changed considerably: in the first place, it is no longer handwoven, and secondly, although some, which is produced in Europe, is still made of linen, the majority of it is now made of cotton. It is also considerably coarser in texture than it was in early days: the canvas used in the twelfth and thirteenth centuries was very fine and had a very pliable, but close weave, which allowed an extensive amount of underside couching with gold thread to be worked.

Modern canvas has a much more rigid nature and a more open weave. Some of the cheaper types of canvas today are made of unpolished cotton which has been stiffened by treating it with size, and quite recently a canvas which is made from a plastic material has been offered to the canvas worker in America. So far this plastic canvas has made little or no progress in England, but, when it can be obtained, it will be found to be useful in the production of three-dimensional, free-standing pieces of embroidery.

There is some confusion as to the exact nature of what is called embroidery, so that it is necessary for us to remember at this stage that true embroidery is what is created by the working of a design upon an existing foundation material, whether it be silk gauze, finely woven open-mesh canvas, closely woven linen or a cotton or woollen fabric. This work has sometimes been called embroidery, sometimes needlework and sometimes — both in the past and also today — tapestry. This last name is really incorrect when applied to a piece of embroidery, as true tapestry is itself a woven material, but over the years the word seems to have been used simply to describe a hanging, even if the work concerned were quite definitely an embroidery.

When considering the uses to which embroidery was put from the earliest times onward, we find that it was always a means of increasing the splendour of important occasions. It was used extensively in the decoration of the sanctuary among the Hebrews. Richly embroidered garments were also worn by the Assyrian and Persian kings, and by the Romans, when seeking to impress, especially during the period of the decline of their great empire. A limitation of its use for religious purposes began during the eighth century AD, when numerous artists and craftsmen, skilled in the production of high quality embroideries, were forced by the intolerance of the Iconoclasts to leave the capital of the former Eastern Empire and come to settle on the banks of the Tiber. The work that these immigrant craftsmen produced in Italy brought a great revival and improvement of embroidery there, but the subject matter of their designs had changed: no longer did they produce work to be used for secular purposes, but everywhere only religious subjects were to be seen, and portraits of the Popes.

It is hard to establish with any certainty the

time at which embroidery of good quality first appeared in Britain. During the period between 1000 BC and 500 BC the Celts arrived and settled here, and their chiefs seem to have had a great love of beautiful things. Many treasures have been found in their graves, including golden torques, bracelets, brooches, shields decorated with vivid enamels, helmets and bronze armour. One of the Celtic characteristics, it has been thought, was vanity, so that embroidered clothing might well have also been included in their buried treasure. No trace of such things has, however, been found, as the burials were of such a nature that fabrics could not have survived in them for such a long time.

During the period from AD 43 to AD 400, when Britain came under the dominance of Rome, examples of embroidery probably came into the country along with all the other luxury goods from the continent, such as glass, perfumeries, mosaics, etc, which followed the marching legionaries along the straight, new Roman roads, but these have likewise not survived to our day.

When the Visigoths sacked Rome in AD 410, the people of Britain were cut off from the civilisation to which they had belonged for nearly four centuries, and the island became a magnet for hoards of wild barbarians, who came to kill and plunder. Very little is known of the events which followed this time, as practically all records were lost in the ensuing chaos, until finally the Angles and Saxons managed to complete the conquest of Britain at the end of the sixth century.

Towards the end of the next century came the first occasion when embroidery in England is mentioned by a contemporary writer. This was when Thomas of Ely referred in the year AD 679 to the fact that Saint Etheldreda, the Abbess of Ely, had offered to Saint Cuthbert a stole and a maniple, a fine and magnificient embroidery in gold and precious stones, worked, it is said, with her own hands, for she was a skilful craftswoman in gold embroidery.[1] At about the same time Aldhelm, the Bishop of Sherborne, referring to the technical skill of the Anglo-Saxon women, says 'The shuttles, not filled with purple only, but with various colours, are pushed here and there among

the thick, spreading threads, and then with the art of embroidery they adorn all the woven work with various groups of figures.[2] It was Saint Aldhelm also who at this time brought back a chasuble with him, when returning from a visit to Rome.

The extent to which English women of those days were occupied with embroidery is shown by the fact that at the Council of Clovesho in the year AD 747 the nuns were told to occupy themselves in reading and singing psalms, rather than in spending so much time in weaving and embroidering robes. It could not have been the aim of the Council to discourage the practice of the art of embroidery in the service of the Church, but rather to enlarge the scriptural knowledge of the people concerned and to improve the quality of their psalm-singing. They may also have considered that the nuns were getting far too much enjoyment from working at their embroidery frames and looms, while, no doubt, passing a great deal of time in chatting and gossiping among themselves, instead of putting their minds to more pious thoughts. Their work might also have led them to become preoccupied with personal adornment.

From early days right up to the sixteenth century it seems to have been usual not only for kings in England to present their coronation robes to the Church but also for the nobles to give their elaborately embroidered mantles, as well as their ordinary wearing apparel. The designs used upon such secular garments at that time were often of a religious nature, so that they would have been very acceptable gifts to the Church. These garments would then be altered to make church vestments, such as copes and chasubles, or they were used to construct a decorative hanging for the altar. The smaller pieces were often made into orphreys, stoles or maniples.

The way in which such early gifts to the Church were adapted for making into church vestments often led to the mutilation of the original design. The truncated figures, roundels and quatrefoils which can be seen, for instance, on the Syon Cope, among others, testify to the lack of consideration for the original design, which was shown, when the embroidered mantles were being adapted to the semi-circular shape of the cope.

There is not much information from the ninth and tenth centuries in England concerning actual pieces of embroidery which were then being made. We do, however, hear that a certain embroiderer, named Eanswitha of Hereford, was granted by the Bishop of Worcester in AD 802 the lease for life of a farm on condition that she undertook to 'renew

---

[1] Thomas of Ely, edited by D J Stewart, *Libra Eliensis* Volume I, page 34, Anglia Christiana, London, 1848.

[2] Christie, AGL, Mrs, *English Medieval Embroidery*, 1938.

Detail of Anglo-Saxon stole, tenth centuy Embroidered in coloured silks — green, blue, red and purple — which have become discoloured over the centuries, and gold thread on a linen ground. This stole, together with a maniple, was found in 1826/7 in the tomb of St Cuthbert in Durham Cathedral. An inscription on the reverse side of both the stole and the maniple records that these were made by order of Aelfflaeda, Queen of Edward the Elder. *Durham Cathedral*

and scour, and from time to time add to, the dresses of the priests who served in the cathedral church.[1] In the library of Durham Cathedral there is a stole and a maniple, embroidered in coloured silks, together with gold thread, on a linen base, and they are lined with silk. These were found in the tomb of Saint Cuthbert in Durham Cathedral in the year 1827 and they are among the most precious relics of Anglo-Saxon art that we possess. It is unusual to find inscriptions or signatures on early work, but both the stole and the maniple have inscriptions at the ends on the reverse side to the effect that they were made by order of Aelfflaeda — who died in 916 — for Bishop

Fridestan, who presided over the See of Winchester from 905 to 933. Aelfflaeda was queen of Edward the Elder (870-924), and her daughters were, according to William of Malmesbury, skilled needlewomen. Saint Cuthbert was the last of the Irish bishops of Lindisfarne, and was later made Bishop of Durham. It appears strange that vestments, specially made for Bishop Fridestan, should be found in the tomb of another saint. Cuthbert had, however, been dearly loved in his lifetime, so that his bones were much revered after his death, and many pilgrims visited his tomb. Among them was King Aethelstan, a stepson of Aelfflaeda, whose name appears on the embroideries in question, and it does not surprise us that he should, on visiting the shrine in 934, make an offering to the Saint, and that, among other things, he should donate the stole and maniple, which had been made by his stepmother for Bishop Fridestan, who had himself died the previous year at Winchester.

Another lady of that time, who is mentioned by name, is Aedelpyrm, who once sent a message to Saint Dunstan requesting him to visit her for the purpose of preparing for her designs for a stole which she was going to make in varied embroidery with gold and gems. Saint Dunstan (924-988) is not likely to have been the only monk who prepared at this time designs for the noble Anglo-Saxon ladies to embroider for the Church. Many monks, who worked in the scriptoria, producing the magnificient illuminated manuscripts of the period, were the most likely people to have prepared designs for embroidery.

If we study both the embroideries themselves and also the social history of the time, it is quite clear that the common people of the land, who were forced to labour constantly at the most menial of tasks in order to sustain a completely wretched state of existence, could not have played any part in the production of such costly objects as embroidered vestments. A mere glance, however, at the contemporary illuminated manuscripts shows us quite clearly that there was a strong link between the designs used there and those employed in working the embroideries. The subjects that are portrayed in the designs, and also the way in which they are developed, that includes the use of decorative details to embellish background areas in both the manuscripts and the embroideries, all point to the calligraphers and illuminators of religious manuscripts as being the same people as those who prepared the designs for works of embroidery.

It was from the time of Saint Dunstan onwards

---

[1]Lambett, A, *Church Needlework*, page 27, London, 1844.

Orphrey for a chasuble (1315-1335) The Tree of Jesse orphrey, which measures 4 ft 9½ in. x 1 ft 2 in. (146 cm x 36 cm), is considered to be the finest, surviving, English mediaeval orphrey. It is worked in coloured silks and silver-gilt thread in underside couching, together with tent and split stitches and raised work on linen. The main subjects depicted are, reading from the bottom upwards, Jesse, David, Solomon, the Virgin and Child and Christ crucified, with the figures of the Virgin and St John appearing on either side of Him *Musée Historique des Tissus, Lyons*

into the eleventh century that a new flowering of Anglo-Saxon culture began. After the complete destruction of the great monastic establishments in the North at Lindisfarne and Jarrow, both of which had been sacked by the Northmen at the end of the eighth century, the main cultural centre in England had moved South into Wessex, which had become a strongly governed kingdom which could develop many fine craftsmen. England began once more to accumulate treasures of gold and silver ornaments and embroidered vestments. The latter were used to adorn not only the dignitaries of the Church but also the nobility themselves who appeared in beautifully embroidered mantles of bright-coloured silk.

It is worthy of note that in Europe also from the end of the tenth century there was a revival in the production of both illuminated manuscripts and embroidery. The break-up of the empire of Charlemagne in the ninth century had been accompanied by a decline in the making of such things, but a great resurgence had occurred at the time of the general revival of monastic culture a century later. New styles of working also emerged at this time, of which the finest were the English and the German. The main characteristic of the English style in illumination was the portrayal of human figures, which were very colourful, vigorous and expressive, set in frames of somewhat heavy ornament, and, although there is very little embroidery of this period still in existence for us to see, we can well believe that it would have been in this same style.

The preparation of the colours for dyeing the materials, which were used in making the embroidered garments of the time, became a mattter of extreme importance in the Middle Ages, and people are known to have travelled great distances to obtain and to study the more famous recipes for dyeing. These they recorded carefully, adding to them and correcting them, as their experience of the dyeing process advanced. In this way the range of colours and the variety of tones of a colour which were available to the embroiderer were greatly increased. All the dyes which were used in those days were obtained from plants and other natural sources, and they gave to the fabrics a bright and beautiful colouring, which enhances in a very lively manner the appearance of mediaeval embroideries, and contrasts strongly with the harsh and garish effect of colours obtained from chemical dyes during the Victorian era.

It must be remembered that during the eleventh century it was still only in the monastic establishments that embroidery was produced. In the world outside the religious houses each small village supplied its own artisans for producing what was required for the life of the community: the smith, the carpenter and the thatcher were given their own holdings in the area in exchange for carrying out whatever work had to be done. Commerce was conducted by means of barter and not by payments of money, since there was very little money available, and it was not until much later that this system gradually gave way to one in which goods could be purchased and work was rewarded by a payment of money. Towns in the modern sense had hardly come into existence by this time, with the exception of London and a few other places. Thus it can be seen that an immense gulf existed between the common people of the land and the members of the religious houses, who were always well-to-do persons, who could afford the materials, such as gold thread and coloured silks and even the needles for working their embroideries, all of which had to be imported from far distant places at enormous expense.

One outstanding person of the eleventh century, who was concerned with the production of works of embroidery, was Margaret, an English princess of the House of Wessex, who was born in Hungary in the year 1045, the daughter of Edward the Exile — himself a son of Edmund Ironside — and Agatha, who is said to have been a kinswoman of Gisela, queen of Saint Stephen of Hungary. Margaret came to England with her parents in 1057, while still a child, but after the Norman Conquest she and her mother, her sister Christine and her brother Edgar Atheling were obliged to flee to Scotland to the court of King Malcolm III. In the year 1070 Margaret married King Malcolm, delightfully known as Canmore (meaning Bighead). He was half Celt and half Dane, but his upbringing and training in Northumbria had made him more of a Northumbrian than a Scot.

Margaret was a very pious and refined lady, and she did much by her example to civilize the northern realm. By her influence on her husband she also helped to guide the northern Church towards the rest of Christendom, especially in regard to such things as the strict observance of the Sabbath, the period of Lent and the Easter communion. In her spare moments it seems that she was also a dedicated embroiderer, for her confessor, a monk named Theodoric, paints a a vivid picture of her workplace, describing it thus: 'Her chamber was like the workshop of a heavenly artist; there copes for singers, chasubles, stoles, altar-cloths and other priestly vestments and church ornaments were always to be seen, some in course of preparation, others, worthy of admiration, already completed'[1] Whether she worked all these things with her own fair hands unaided is a matter for conjecture, but I think we can be pretty sure that many other hands were pressed into service in the production of these articles of rare beauty for the adornment of the church. In addition to performing her pious duties and producing embroidery, she was also associated with her husband in having a church built at Dunfermline, and it has been suggested that she re-founded the monastic institution at Iona. All this, as well as bearing her husband six sons and two daughters.

Malcolm was killed in 1093 and Margaret died just three days later, at the age of 48 years, apparently from the shock at her husband's death. She was canonised in the year 1250.

From details of information which have come down to us concerning Agatha, the mother of Saint Margaret of Scotland, it appears that there was a close relationship between her and Gisela, the wife of Saint Stephen, the first Christian king of Hungary. Saint Stephen, who died in 1038, was zealous, not only for the temporal good of his people, but, above all, for their conversion from the worship of idols to the Christian religion. He was also exceedingly interested in the art of embroidery and encouraged his wife Gisela to set up and organise weaving and embroidery workshops in the vicinity of the palace in order to produce the vestments and other ecclesiastical embroideries needed for the decoration of the churches. It has been suggested that it was from Gisela's workshop that the celebrated canvas work stitch-pattern, known as *point d' Hongrie*, originated.[2] Hungarian stitch, as we now call it, is

---

[1] *De Sancta Scotiae Regina, in Acta Sanctorum Junii*, Vol. II, page 329, Antwerp, 1698.

[2] Lefébure, Ernest, *Embroidery and Lace* page 65, London, 1889.

still in use today, but it has acquired in the course of time numerous other names, such as Florentine, Flame and — more recently — Bargello stitch.

Although there is a degree of uncertainty concerning the exact nature of many of the very early embroideries, one piece, which has been in existence for over eight hundred years, can still actually be seen. This is the famous Bayeux Tapestry which is so important a piece in the general history of embroidery that it should be mentioned here, although it is not an example of canvas work. It is a long, narrow panel, measuring 231 ft x 19½ in. (70 m x 50 cm), and is worked in stem stitch and laid stitch on a coarse linen ground in wool of two kinds. Unfortunately, the final part of this remarkable record of the Norman Conquest is now missing, but sufficient of the original work remains to give us a very good idea of the type of secular embroidery which was being done in England in the second half of the eleventh century.

As we have already noticed, the word 'tapestry' was a general term used in early days to designate all types of hanging whether they were actual woven tapestry, canvas work or, as in this case, crewel-work embroidery. This particular piece of embroidery has always been known as the Bayeux Tapestry, and it would be presumptuous for anyone to suggest changing its title now to indicate that it was not a woven piece.

The precise date and place of origin of the Bayeux Tapestry are not known, but it is thought to be English work and to have been produced within twenty years of the Norman invasion of England. It was probably commissioned by Bishop Odo, the half-brother of William of Normandy, to be hung in the nave of his new cathedral at Bayeux.

When one examines examples of embroidery produced at this time, it is sometimes difficult to be sure whether they are of English or French origin. German and Italian work of the period can always be easily separated from English examples, but this cannot be done with certainty when a piece of presumed French origin is compared with the English. This is considered to be due to the fact that France and England enjoyed a close relationship during the early Middle Ages, which was itself based upon the close connection that existed between the royal house of England and the nobility of France. In describing the arts and crafts of the twelfth century there has even been a reference to them as belonging to the School of the English Channel.[1]

Among pieces of early English embroidery,

which have survived to this day, the Bayeux Tapestry is unique in portraying contemporary events. Most of the other early work depicts religious subjects but we know that there were also some secular embroideries which recorded deeds of valour on the field of battle. One such piece was a hanging made at the order of a lady named Aethelflaed and given by her to Ely Minster to honour the memory of her husband, Byrhtnoth, who was killed at the battle of Maldon in 991. This particular hanging is described in an inventory as a woven curtain, but experts think it is more likely to have been embroidered.

It is interesting to note that in 1808 the Bayeux Tapestry was sent on a tour of France by order of Napoleon Bonaparte, and that it was exhibited in the theatres of Paris. Napoleon had persuaded himself that, by publicising one conquest of England, he could evoke enthusiasm for another, but he became less keen on the hanging when he saw the scene depicting King Harold's fear at the appearance of a comet, because it predicted his defeat. A meteor is said to have been seen in the South of France at that time, and Napoleon regarded it as a most unlucky omen, as, in fact, it proved to be.

The period of the Crusades

From as far back as the seventh century AD it had been the custom for certain individuals from the West to go on pilgrimages to the Holy Land. These were always peaceful in nature, until in 1071 the Seljuk Turks overthrew the army defending Byzantium, captured the Emperor and brought persecution and suffering to the Western pilgrims as they made their way towards Jerusalem. This was a bitter blow to Christianity in the East, and it aroused a wave of intense feeling against the infidel. As a result, a vast crusading movement was initiated, which spurred the Christian armed forces of Western Europe into considerable activity, which lasted for over two hundred years. Numerous bands of nobles, clad in armour, set out to fight the Saracens, and to keep the way open for the Christian pilgrims to go to Palestine. On their return home, these crusaders were dressed in the rich fabrics they had plundered from the East. They brought back not only splendid costumes for themselves but also caparisons for their horses,

---

[1] James, Philip, *English Mediaeval Art* in 'The Collector', June, 1930.

pouches and many other richly embroidered objects. It is no wonder that the needleworkers of the West eyed these embroideries with enormous interest and were spellbound with admiration at the sight of such richness, as they were also at the tales of the many wondrous things the crusaders had seen on their journeys, the splendours of Constantinople and of other towns of Asia Minor.

The Fourth Crusade, which began in 1202, was undertaken by groups of mainly Flemish and Italian nobles. They attacked and finally, in 1204, occupied the city of Constantinople, which they plundered of its accumulation of treasures. These included gold and silver ware, as well as cloth of gold and other ancient materials, together with Byzantine embroideries. The treasury of Halberstadt in the German Democratic Republic still contains certain ancient Byzantine embroideries which, it is thought, have been held there since they were obtained in this early conquest of Constantinople.

There must have been many other examples of such pieces of embroidery having been brought back to the West from Constantinople, as we know that the crusaders, on returning home after years of absence, often gave thanks to God for their safe return by making offerings to the churches of plunder acquired on their travels, such as richly embroidered materials which would have been very suitable for use on great occasions.

Opus Anglicanum

A good result of the Crusades was the widening of knowledge in the West concerning the art of other lands, and particularly of Oriental and Byzantine art. This had a profound influence upon our native designers and embroiderers and undoubtedly led them on to their greatest achievement in those works of unsurpassable beauty, which were produced during the thirteenth and fourteenth centuries and are known as *Opus Anglicanum*. A few fragments of some embroidered vestments, which were found in 1861 in the stone coffin of Bishop Walter de Cantelupe in Worcester Cathedral, are thought to reveal the first suggestion of the special technique which is a characteristic of *Opus Anglicanum*, and they were probably worked during the first half of the thirteenth century.

From that time onwards, until it reached its peak in the middle of the fourteenth century — the years 1307 to 1377 are usually quoted as the period of highest achievement — *Opus Anglicanum*

Detail of Bayeux Tapestry   This section shows the scene in which King Harold expresses his fear at the appearance of a comet

became the most important element in embroidery anywhere in the mediaeval world. No other artistic product of this country ever aroused such great acclaim, and examples of this work were constantly sought after by all the greatest princes and nobles of Europe. In the Vatican inventory of 1295 far more pieces of English work are listed than are any other types of embroidery.

Although some amateur needleworkers, such as queens and ladies in the great houses and in convents, were concerned in its production, it is now generally accepted that the main bulk of *Opus Anglicanum* was done by professional embroiderers, who carried on their craft principally in well-organised workshops in the City of London. This work was generally administrated by men, but the actual embroiderers were both men and women, who had been trained for the

purpose by serving an apprenticeship of seven years duration.

All the examples of *Opus Anglicanum* which are still in existence are embroidered ecclesiastical vestments, which have been preserved in the Church or by patrons of the Church. Nothing remains of any secular embroidered garments of the time, apart from the surcoat of Edward the Black Prince, a replica of which can be seen hanging above his tomb in Canterbury Cathedral. The original, unfortunately, is nothing more than a collection of tattered remnants, but it was, no doubt, originally very similar in appearance to the ecclesiastical garments which still survive, as were also the vast numbers of other articles of secular clothing and home furnishings, decorated with embroidery, for the existence of which we have plenty of written evidence, even if the ravages of time have destroyed the actual pieces of embroidery themselves.

One of the most beautiful pieces of work belonging to the best period of *Opus Anglicanum* is the famous Syon Cope, which is now kept with several other fine examples of this particular type

Part of an altar frontal or dossal (1315-1335)   with scenes from the Passion of Christ. The scene on the left shows Christ's Charge to Peter, and that on the right the Betrayal. A missing third scene was probably the Flagellation *British Museum*, London

Fragments of a vestment found in 1861 in a tomb at Worcester Cathedral, which was thought to be that of Walter de Cantelupe, Bishop of Worcester 1236-66

of embroidery in the Victoria and Albert Museum in London. It is thought to have been made at some time between the years 1300 and 1320 and is still in a remarkable state of preservation after more than six and a half centuries. A wealthy guild, or some other patron of the monastery of Syon at Isleworth, which had been built and endowed in the years 1414 to 1415 by Henry V for the nuns of Saint Bridget's order, donated the cope to the monastery. When a troubled time for the nuns at Syon occurred at the beginning of the reign of Queen Elizabeth I, they fled abroad, taking the beautiful cope with them. They wandered around in Flanders and France and finally came to rest in Portugal, where the Syon Cope is said to have remained until it was brought back to England in 1810. Subsequently it passed into the possession of the Earl of Shrewsbury, among others, before finally being purchased by the Victoria and Albert Museum in 1864.

When one studies the method of working which was adopted by the skilled embroiderers in producing these famous pieces of *Opus Anglicanum* embroidery, it appears that split stitch was almost exlusively used for working the figures depicted upon them. This stitch was employed to work both the flesh and the draperies, and the background was worked with silver-gilt thread in underside couching. An outstanding characteristic of this type of embroidery is the method by which

Another fragment found in the tomb at Worcester, which was thought to be that of Walter de Cantelup, Bishop of Worcester 1236-66.

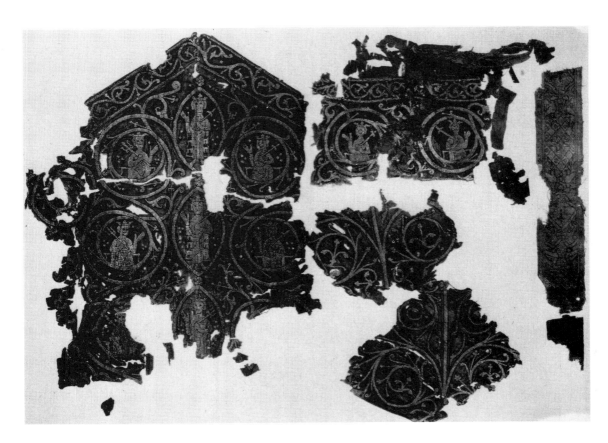

Fragments of a vestment found in 1861 in a tomb at Worcester Cathedral, which was thought to be that of Walter de Cantelupe, Bishop of Worcester 1236-66. Worked with silver-gilt and silk thread in underside couching and stem stitch.
All the above fragments at the British Museum, London

the faces have been worked. A fine silk thread was brought up from the back of the embroidery to the surface at a point just below the centre of the cheek bone, and split stitch was worked with it around this point in a very close spiral, until the stitches reached a position from which the thread could conveniently be taken around the outside contour of the face, and the lower part of the cheek was then worked by placing lines of split stitch side by side to cover the area concerned. Some writers[1] maintain that the spiral shapes, which had been worked upon the cheeks, were forced down into hollows by means of a small iron instrument with a knob on the end, which was slightly heated and then pressed down upon

the work, but the mere working of split stitch in such very close spirals could well have produced this effect automatically.

A further remarkable and characteristic feature of *Opus Anglicanum* is its method of couching down threads, whether of metal, such as gold or silver, or of silk. The thread, which was to be couched down, was placed upon the surface of the background material, which was a type of fine linen canvas, and it was caught down at intervals by means of a length of linen thread, held on the underside of the background material. The needle containing the couching thread was brought up through this material at the required point of fixing, taken over the gold, silver or silk thread on the surface and back down again through the same hole as that from which it had emerged. A tiny loop of the thread to be couched down was then pulled down through the background material. (See diagram (a) page 21.)

The variety of other stitches used in these early embroideries was very limited, and it is interesting to note that all of them are still in use today. Tent stitch, satin stitch and long and short stitch appear

[1] Rock, Dr Daniel *Textile Fabrics*, 1870.

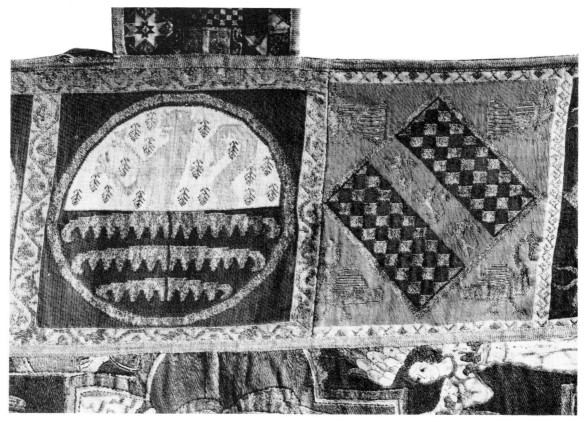

Syon Cope   Detail of orphrey see also colour plate 1
Victoria and Albert Museum, London

upon a frontal for an altar as early as 1290, and on a burse of the same date cross stitch and plait stitch were used. On one of the best-preserved of English mediaeval embroideries, the Pienza Cope (Capitole della Cathedrale di Pienza) of 1315-1335, tent stitch, satin stitch and overcast stitch are used in conjuction with split stitch and underside couching. The Corporation of London possesses two seal bags, dated 1319, which show heraldic designs and are worked in split stitch, cross stitch, two-sided Italian stitch and eyelet stitch, together with underside couching. It would appear that this is the earliest known example of the use of two-sided Italian and eyelet stitches.

The backgrounds of this early embroidery, on which underside couching of the gold thread was used, show that the working was done mainly in the form of brick patterns in the earliest examples, changing in the thirteenth century to chevron patterns, which were later developed into various square and diamond shapes.

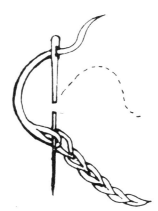

Sketch of split stitch

When we examine the designs used in *Opus Anglicanum* pieces, we note that the human figures portrayed show considerable variation from one to another in stature and general appearance, but that, in the main, they are all somewhat shorter than those depicted in the work of other European nations at this time and are very different from the

Opus Anglicanum Sketch showing the method of
working faces spirally in silk split stitch

Sketch showing method used for couching gold thread
(a) *Underside couching* (b) *Surface couching*

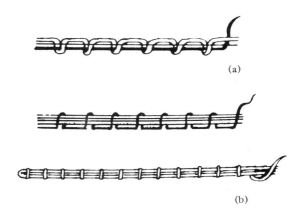

(a)

(b)

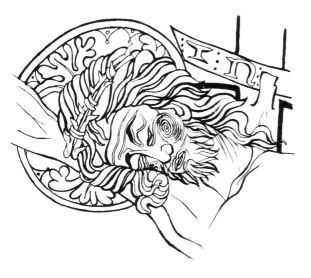

The Melk Chasuble Sketch showing the method of
working faces spirally in silk split stitch

Pienza Cope (detail) 1315-35 This cope, which measures
5 ft 4½in. x 11 ft 6 in. (1.6 m x 3.5 m) is one of the best-
preserved of English mediaeval embroideries. It is worked
on linen with silver and silver-gilt thread and coloured
silk in underside couching, split, tent, satin and overcast
stitches. Originally it was adorned with many pearls,
which have now unhappily disappeared.
Capitolo della Cattedrale di Pienza

exaggeratedly tall and impressive figures of the
Byzantine period. They generally appear to have
rather large heads, hands and feet and a mass of
dark hair surrounding a pale face. The areas of
split stitch, worked spirally on the cheeks, give a
hollowed appearance to the faces, which have protruding eyes and, in the case of the men, clean-

shaven mouths and prominent chins, fringed with a slight beard. There is nothing about either the facial expression or the bodily attitudes that could be described as idealistic, but the figures are dramatically posed, with their hands making extremely expressive gestures to indicate supplication, surprise or argument. The saints hold their respective symbols boldly at arm's length and point at them with their free hand, as if insisting upon recognition.

Every single element in the design, whether it is a human figure, or that of a beast or a bird, or a representation of natural foliage or flowers, is intensely alive and vivacious. The scenes depicted are also dramatic, with the saints represented in them being fully recognisable, and yet the whole composition remains essentially decorative rather than pictorial.

All these early vestments, in which the entire surface is covered with needlework, are embroidered upon a linen foundation which was invariably used two-fold and consisted of a coarse linen background with a finer linen placed on top, the embroidery stitches being taken through both layers. This method of working was probably used in order to give greater firmness to the work and to support the weight of the gold-thread embroidery better. This is understandable, as the linen of those days was so very fine, when compared with the material we use at the present time.

Small articles such as purses, pouches, seal bags, burses and book covers

In addition to the embroidering of ecclesiastical and secular vestments, the period of the *Opus Anglicanum* was also a time when a similar kind of canvas work was used for embellishing such things as book covers, and bags and purses of various types. Pouches and purses were worn suspended from belts or girdles and became very popular during the Crusades, when they were used for carrying small items such as gloves, money, prayerbooks and any other valuable articles, which needed to be transported around by the wearer. Most of these small bags were embroidered with their owner's heraldic device and were all beautifully trimmed in some way, either with ornamental tassles, made of metal or silk thread, or with bobbles of silk. Occasionally some would even be hung with small bells. Such objects remained popular for very many years, and it is interesting to note that several pouches and purses, which

The front of a Seal Bag, showing the figure of St Paul on the arms of the City of London. This bag serves to protect the Great Seal on a charter dated 8 June, 1319. This is a rare case in which a very early piece of embroidery can be accurately dated. The work is done with silver and silver-gilt thread and coloured silks in underside couching, using split, cross and two-sided Italian cross stitches on an even-weave linen. The whole bag is 5 in. (12.7 cm) in diameter
The Corporation of London, Guildhall

The reverse side of the Seal Bag, showing the royal arms of England, which are flanked by two wyverns and have three crowns above. The background of the royal arms is particularly interesting, as it is worked entirely in eyelet stitches, which must make this piece one of the earliest known examples of an embroidery in which this stitch is used *The Corporation of London, Guildhall*

Opus Anglicanum   Sketch of the figure of Daniel on the Tree of Jesse Orphrey for a chasuble

Opus Anglicanum   Sketch of the figure of Moses from a cope in the Cathedral of St Bertrand de Comminges

Opus Anglicanum   Sketch of the figure of King David on the Tree of Jesse Orphrey for a chasuble

Opus Anglicanum   Details sketched from the same cope in the Cathedral of St Bertrand, showing an angel and birds

Opus Anglicanum   Sketch of the Virgin in the Coronation scene from a cope in the Cathedral of St Bertrand de Comminges (1300-1320)

Opus Anglicanum   Sketch of the figure of St Catherine from a cope in the Museo Civico, Pienza

Burse English fourteenth century, worked with coloured silks in tent and cross stitch on fine linen
Victoria and Albert Museum, London

were made during the thirteenth and fourteenth centuries, bear the coats of arms of foreign families, while at the same time showing definite signs of being English work, a fact which points to the existence in England at that time of an extensive export trade in such articles.

Among other examples of small pieces of embroidery of this type is a corporal case belonging to Wymondham Abbey in Norfolk, England,

which is said to date from the early fourteenth century. It shows on each side three shields of arms in rectangular compartments and is worked in plait stitch with coloured silks on linen. Further similar pieces, which can be seen at the Victoria and Albert Museum, are, in addition to various purses and pouches, two seal bags on a charter of 1319 and some burses. Some of the latter show coats of arms worked in embroidery, but it was

Opus Anglicanum Thirteenth century burse showing the Crucifixion and the Coronation of the Virgin, embroidered on linen with silver-gilt thread and split stitch
Victoria and Albert Museum, London

24

Purse, English 1290-1340 On each side of the purse are four rows of four shields, worked alternately on squares of green and red. Each shield is repeated, and the arms they bear are thought to be the following: starting from the top on one side are Austrasier and Blois, Burgundy and one unknown, England and Warras and Monfaucon de Montebeliard and Brittany; on the other side are County of Geneva and Lorraine, von Tann? and one unknown, de Hulgonet and Montbeliard and Burgundy and France. This purse is probably one of the English embroidered purses, which were exported to the continent of Europe in large numbers at that time. It is worked in coloured silks in long-legged cross (plait) stitch on linen. The size is 7 in. x 6 in. (17.7 cm x 15.2 cm) *Germanisches National-Museum, Nürnberg*

more usual for them to have depicted on one side the head of Christ or Christ crucified, together with the figures of the Virgin Mary and Saint John, and on the other side the Lamb of God or the Coronation of the Virgin, with stars, rosettes, peacocks and eagles sprinkled over the background.

During the late thirteenth and early fourteenth centuries embroidery was also used for working the covers of precious Bibles, Psalters and Books of Hours. The earliest known example of such an embroidered binding, which is still in existence and is kept in the British Museum, is the one which is attached to the Felbrigge Psalter. The Annunciation is depicted on the front cover and the Crucifixion on the back, both being worked in split stitch on fine linen with floss silk of various colours, and with fine gold thread surface couched in a chevron pattern forming the background. The extraordinary fineness of the gold thread can be fully realised, when it is seen that 10 threads of gold, couched closely side by side, cover approximately $\frac{1}{8}$ in. (3 mm) in width.

Whether the two embroidered panels used on this binding were designed specifically for the Psalter in question is something it is difficult to ascertain with certainty. We know that it was not until the second half of the fourteenth century that the Psalter came into the possession of Anne, the daughter of Sir Simon Felbrigge, KG, who was a nun in the convent of Minoresses at Bruisyard in Suffolk, and an old note inside the book itself states that, after the death of Sister Anne Felbrigge, it remained in the care of the Convent of Bruisyard.[1] The manuscript itself is, however, of a considerably earlier date than the late fourteenth century and is thought to have been written about

a century before, probably in 1280. The panels of embroidery are difficult to date, as they are now in a very poor condition, and suggestions as to their probable date of origin vary from the time when the manuscript was written in the thirteenth century up to the first quarter of the fourteenth century, and there has also been a suggestion that they were worked by Anne Felbrigge herself.[2] It has, however, been maintained that the panels show every sign of being the work of professional embroiderers and were, therefore, considerably older than the late fourteenth century.[3]

Canvas work in Germany — Opus Teutonicum

Embroidery as an art form has long held an important position in Germany, and from the early Middle Ages right up to the eighteenth century every kind of woven material was used as a foundation for this work. As in England, no specimen from very early times has survived, but records show that in the eight century noble

[1] Dryden, Alice, *Church Embroidery*, page 40, The Arts of the Church Series, London, 1911.

[2] Kendrick, A F *English Embroidery*, page 48, London, 1904.

[3] Lethaby, W R *Proceedings of the Society of Antiquaries*, 2 nd Series, Vol XXI.

Corporal case, early fourteenth century   This case consists of two pieces of coarse linen canvas, each measuring about 9 in.(22.8 cm) square, which are worked with silk in long-legged cross stitch, a stitch which was in common use in those days. The design is formed by dividing the area to be worked horizontally at a point two thirds of the way down. The top part is divided vertically into three equal panels, each containing a stylised tree growing from a pointed mound. The lower area contains three coats of arms, and four of the shields shown belong to families, which held lands in Norfolk, de Warenne, Gurney, Molintune and Bigod. The other two are unidentifiable   *Wymondham Abbey, now the Parish Church of Wymondham, near Norwich*

A maniple,   worked in long-legged cross stitch in silk on fine linen canvas. This maniple, which is dated 1290-1340, shows eighteen shields placed on alternate squares of green and faded red, and is 4 ft 2 in. long x 2 in. to 2½ in. wide (127 cm x 5-6 cm), the width increasing to 3½ in. (8.9 cm) at the ends. It is related to the stole and maniple, which were used to form the semi-circular orphrey of the Syon Cope   *Victoria and Albert Museum, London*

The Felbrigge Psalter, thirteenth century   It is not ▷ known when this embroidered binding was worked, but it is thought to be somewhat later than the manuscript, and probably dates from the early fourteenth century. It is generally believed to be the oldest known example of an embroidered binding in existence
British Museum, London

ladies in Germany donated embroideries of their own making to churches and monastries. It was probably in the eleventh century that embroidery reached such a high level in that part of Europe, that it began to be valued as equal to the precious examples of this work, which had been imported from Middle Eastern countries. Beginning as early as the end of the twelfth century and continuing until the fourteenth, a special kind of embroidery can be recognised which is peculiar to Germany and which is mentioned by mediaeval writers as *Opus Teutonicum*. This work which shows, in fact, the very beginnings of canvas work in Germany, is quite unlike anything produced in England at that time, and it is certainly very different from modern canvas embroidery.

Opus Teutonicum included two different types of technique, one in which the design was simply outlined with chain stitch, and the other which was used mainly for altar pieces, and which is of greater interest to us, where the whole surface of the background material was covered with a large variety of stitches, worked in diaper patterns. The foundation material, which was used in this work, was a white canvas-like linen, and this was embroidered entirely with pure white linen thread in a flat style with no attempt at moulding or shading in any way. It may have been the absence of

colour in this work which led to the introduction at this time of many new stitches with the object of relieving the monotony that the lack of colour had occasioned: the directional use of stitches and the change from one stitch to another would act as a substitute for changes of colour.

Buttonhole, basket, encroaching Gobelin and Long-legged cross appear to be the main stitches used, while split stitch, so beloved by the English at this time, running or satin stitch were never used, as far as can be ascertained, and it is exceedingly rare to find examples even of the simple cross stitch. These stitches were used to give the maximum effect, and they formed delightful zigzag, lozenge, diamond and chevron patterns.

German embroiderers continued to use stitch patterns right up to the fifteenth century, but the former high standard of work began to decline, when in the fourteenth century coloured silks were used together with the white threads on the white line ground. These silks were first used only to outline the shapes to be worked, but before long they had completely replaced the white thread. As might now be expected, this increase in the use of colour was followed by a decline in the variety of the stitches used. Gobelin stitch, which is a simple, straight stitch, was the only one to survive the change.

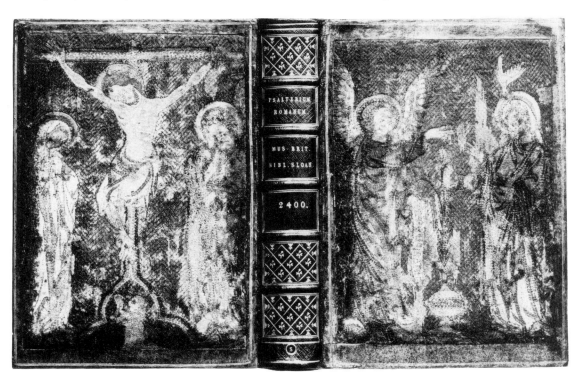

Fragment of an altar cloth of the late fourteenth century
This is German work from Westphalia and consists of
white linen embroidered in chain stitch with white linen
thread   *Victoria and Albert Museum, London*

Detail of the Hildesheim Cope,   German, mid fourteenth
century   *Victoria and Albert Museum, London*

Detail of designs on a Cope in Göss, Styria This is twelfth to thirteenth century German work, and the entire surface of the canvas-like linen used is covered with these geometric designs, which are worked in a fine chain stitch with different coloured silks. The all-over pattern of the entire surface gives the effect of a woven fabric.

It is interesting to note that just as a 'Gild of Broderers' was developed in England during the Middle Ages, Germany also had a secular guild of embroiderers, called the *Gold und Seidennater*, which is mentioned in the records of the Cologne Corporation in the fourteenth century.

From the middle of the sixteenth century and throughout the seventeenth century there was a decline both in the style and in the amount of amateur work produced in Germany. Embroidery throughout Europe was influenced at this time

A German hanging of the early sixteenth century This large hanging was embroidered at the convent of Heningen, near Hanover. It is worked on canvas in coloured worsteds *Victoria and Albert Museum, London*

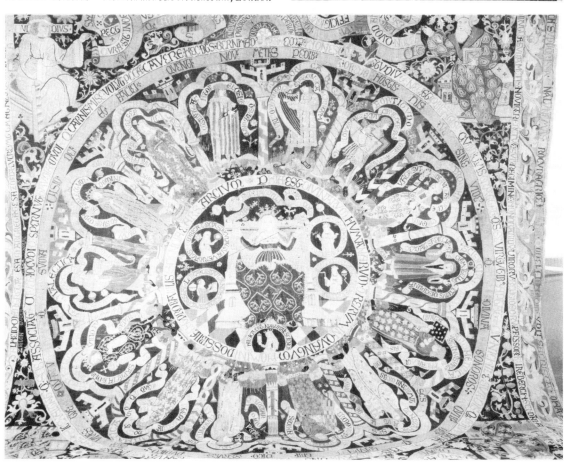

more and more by the Italian Renaissance, which caused it to develop into a purely decorative art, dominated, as were all other branches of the decorative arts, by the influence of Italian grotesques. Even the technicalities of the various crafts were influenced, so that national elements in embroidery merged gradually into one international style.

Germany's main contribution to the history of canvas work at this time was probably made not so much in its embroideries as in its printed books. These new books did a great deal to publicise and to popularise the patterns of the Italian Renaissance, and it was their influence, as well as their wide availability to a large number of people, which started the main interest in sampler-making during the sixteenth and seventeenth centuries. All the little scenes, the houses, scrolls, flowers, animals and insects, as well as the alphabets themselves, were copied direct from these early printed books by all the keen amateur embroiderers in Europe.

The decline from the excellence of English mediaeval embroidery

As we have already noted, the highly acclaimed English embroidery, known as *Opus Anglicanum*, is thought to have reached its highest peak in the years between 1307 and 1377. Thereafter a gradual decline in the standard of the work is noticeable. This has been ascribed to a variety of causes, such as the prolonged foreign and civil wars of the time, and the social and economic troubles occasioned by that dreadful and devastating plague, known as the Black Death, which reached England from continental Europe in the middle of the fourteenth century, and recurred at intervals during the next twenty years and more, wiping out enormous numbers of people, among whom must have been many skilled embroiderers, as well as other craftsmen.

It is interesting to note further that the art of illumination also experienced a decline during this period, which is what one would expect, when it is realised that the persons who designed the embroideries were also those who had produced the illuminated manuscripts. Ever since the embroiderer had become a professional and carried on his craft in a workshop, the drawing of the designs had been the province of artists, who were at first illuminators and calligraphers, and later painters — except, of course, in the case of the occasional nun or wealthy lady, who preferred to design her own piece of work. Generally the designs

were either purchased by the manufacturer, or supplied to the workshop by the client. These designs usually became the property of the embroiderers after the piece of work was completed, and they were then free to copy or alter a design as they thought fit. It is, therefore, quite understandable that, when the economic situation became difficult, the producers of this work would naturally look around for ways of economising and would utilise the old, wornout designs already in the workshop, rather than employ a hightly-paid designer to produce new ideas. These old designs would then have been transferred to the linen by workers, who were inexperienced in drawing, and would, as a result, have lost at least half of the true nature of the original design in the process.

A further decline in the standard of workmanship in embroidery in England at this time resulted from the fact that during the first half of the fifteenth century the well-tried method of underside couching was replaced by a newer, simpler and cheaper method of surface couching. As a result, the finished piece of embroidery was far less flexible and much more vulnerable to wear and tear, as the thread, which was used for couching down a thread of gold, remained on the surface of the work, instead of being placed safely on the back out of harm's way, as in the older method of working.

The strict supervision of the embroidery workshops was also relaxed at this time; fines for poor workmanship were abolished and pieces of work were no longer destroyed, if they fell below an accepted standard, as had been the case in former days.

Fragment of a German embroidery of the fifteenth century
This piece is worked in cross stitch over one intersection
of the canvas *Victoria and Albert Museum, London*

Then, in addition to all this, a change of fashion
occurred, which led to further problems for the
embroiderers: new woven fabrics, such as figured
silk brocades, satin damasks, velvets and cloth of
gold, were imported from Italy and Spain and
became very popular for use in the making of
vestments of various kinds. Among these new
materials the sumptuous velvet fabrics presented
the greatest problem to the English embroideres,
because it is quite impossible to embrider satisfactorily upon a pile surface. They eventually
dealt with this problem, however, by working the
religious figures, symbols or heraldic devices on
the old canvas-type linen as usual and then applying
them to the background by stitching them on to
the new velvet material.

Applied embroidery naturally gives a very slight
raised effect to the finished work, which distin-
guishes it from work actually carried out on a
single basic fabric. In some cases also, where one
or two layers of the linen were placed on top
of the velvet, the working of the embroidery
was taken through both the linen and the velvet.
The surplus linen then had to be cut away closely
around the edges of the embroidered areas, when
the work was completed, and often a cord was
applied to cover up the cut edge.

German whitework   This piece is thought to have been
produced between 1720 and 1740
Victoria and Albert Museum, London

31

A new method of working had been evolved, and the cost of production had probably been more than halved by eliminating the very long and time-consuming process of working the background, but the painstaking and superb craftsmanship of the previous era had been lost; it was replaced by a cheaper, more theatrically showy and spectacular technique.

Detail of a chasuble of the late fourteenth century, showing the Archangel Gabriel, which is in the Cathedral of St Elisabeth in Kosice in Czechoslovakia

The development of canvas work

The English embroidery workshops had during the fifteenth century become fully commercially orientated and had begun to operate in a rather different manner from previously. They were now working on a mass-production basis and had simplified their techniques by producing innumerable identical motifs — floral motifs, pineapple motifs, fleur-de-lys and motifs depicting various angels — which were all worked and cut out and then kept ready to be applied to any chosen background fabric. Orders for pieces of work were now obtained by sending out representatives from the workshops, rather than by merely awaiting commissions from wealthy clients.

There was much competition at this time from embroidery workshops in Flanders, and this may well have caused the change in the way of working in England. It is interesting to note that it was from Flanders that a different type of couching, known as *or nué*, was introduced into this country in the later fifteenth century and the early sixteenth century. This is a method of surface couching, in which the gold thread is held down by means of coloured silks to produce the necessary shading effect required when working nimbuses and draperies. The silk stitches are worked in varying density over the gold thread, being denser where more shade is to be indicated, and less dense where high-lights are needed. Only a small amount of this particular type of work appears to have been produced in England, however, in spite of the fact that Flemish embroiderers are known to have been working here at that time.

Another important element of change which occurred in the fifteenth century was one that affected education and, through it, helped the development of the middle classes in this country. Since the time of Chaucer little had changed in the social life of the people of England, but during the fifteenth century there was an increase in educational facilities, which resulted from the building of numerous schools and colleges. It was now possible, not only for the sons of the gentry to go to such an institution, and to study Latin — a necessary subject for anyone in those days wishing to take up a professional career — but also for the ablest of the sons of the burghers and yeomen to enjoy a similar education. This great increase in educational facilities for the young men of that time led on to the building up of the middle classes in England.

One member of this new fifteenth century middle class was William Caxton (1422-1491), who brought into this country from Flanders in 1477 the first printing machine. He was a successful merchant of the Mercers Livery Company of London, and for thirty years he lived in the Low Countries, where he made sufficient money to enable him to spend his later years in the study of literature and in translating French books into English. During his time abroad he became interested in the new process of printing with moveable type, which he studied not only in Bruges, but also in Cologne. When he returned to England, Caxton set up his press at Westminster, where he produced during the last fourteen years of his life a large number of books, mainly in the English language. He little realised how greatly the advent of his printing press would influence people's lives by providing a much easier access to knowledge of all kinds in the form of printed books. The printed word became the great weapon of political and religious controversy, which was to alter forever the shape of religion in England, and, in the period after the dissolution of the monasteries, it was from illustrations in the new books that people like embroiderers were to find ideas for designs for new pieces of work. Pattern books now replaced the manuscripts of earlier days as the sources of design material for embroidery. Herbals, bestiaries and other books containing botanical drawings and drawings of animals made it much easier for the lay person to copy the shape of a chosen animal or flower, either by using the picture exactly as printed, or by adapting it to fit a specific space. Some of the more famous printed pattern books of the sixteenth century were Konrad Gesner's *Catalogues Plantarum* (1542) and his *Historia Animalium* (several editions between 1551 and 1558), both of which were published in Zürich, Claude Paradin's *Devises Héroiques* (1557), which was published in Lyons and was used by Mary, Queen of Scots, when working on the Oxburgh Panels, and John Gerard's *Herball* which was published in England in 1597.

Mention should be made here not only of the printed pattern books which provided designs for amateurs to use in embroidery, but also of a new writing instrument, which was produced at this time. This was a graphite pencil, which could be used to write and draw on paper, and which replaced the so-called 'silver point' previously used. The new pencil produced a line which was deeper in tone than that which had been achieved before, and which could be varied much more. It also had the great advantage that a line drawn with it could be easily corrected and was capable of being entirely erased.

This new writing instrument was first mentioned in 1564 by Johann Mathesius, and in the following year Gesner, whose name we have already noticed in connection with the production of printed pattern books, described a wooden holder which was then being used to contain the stick of graphite. It was not until 1795, however, when France was unable to obtain graphite from the English mines at Borrowdale, that a French chemist, Nicholas-Jacques Conté, solved the problem of producing pencils with varying degrees of hardness or softness, and pencils, as we know them today, first came into being.

Funeral palls

All secular embroidery prior to that of the late fifteenth century has disappeared, but from that date onwards there are still in existence some magnificently embroidered funeral palls, hearse covers or 'beryall cloths', many of which belong to several of the great Livery Companies of the City of London. These very well-preserved pieces form a valuable link between the earlier purely ecclesiastical work and the later secular pieces. They may also be said to hold this intermediary position because of the fact that, although they are in the possession of purely secular institutions, they were designed for use in a religious ceremony. Such funeral palls, which were a symbol of continuity, fellowship and sympathy, must have been deemed a necessity at this time, as not only the great Livery Companies and wealthy merchants owned them, but also almost every guild or fraternity, and each parish and municipality possessed one — and in many cases more than one. Saint Margaret's, Westminster charged eight pence for the hiring of theirs.

Whilst some of these funeral palls consisted simply of a plain, rectangular piece of material, others were very elaborate works of art. Often they were made with lappets to cover the sides of the coffin, and these side-panels were usually embroidered with the coats-of-arms of the guilds or cities they represented, or with those of the various wealthy merchants who owned them, and often inscriptions were incorporated in the design. The palls belonging to the famous Livery Companies have mostly a central panel of cloth of gold with a woven pattern of a wavy stem with conventional flowers and leaves in velvet pile and gold loops, a material which was probably imported at a high price from Florence. The four side-panels were often of a contrasting colour in velvet, embroidered throughout and generally edged with gold and silk fringes. The embroidered parts were worked by placing a piece of fine linen, on to which the design was traced, upon the surface of the velvet, and working through both thicknesses of material with coloured silks and gold thread, and sometimes using sequins as well.

Specific examples of the funeral palls of the late fifteenth and early sixteenth centuries include that of the Saddlers' Company, which is thought to be the oldest of all the City Livery Companies. This is an extremely beautiful pall, which is still laid on the table, when a new member is sworn, as a token of the vacancy. The central panel is of red velvet, probably from Italy, which has a woven pattern in gold thread and gold loops, depicting vases with flowers and foliage. The four side-panels are also of red velvet, and upon each of them is embroidered a scene, showing the Assumption of the Virgin. This is flanked by columns and coats-of-arms, which are suspended from a helping hand, protruding from a cloud. The remaining space on each of the two long side-panels is filled with an inscription, taken from the concluding phrases of the *Te Deum*. The whole pall is surrounded by a fringe of gold thread and silk. It is interesting to note that in the immediate Post-Reformation period the figure of the Virgin was cleverly concealed by the application over it of small panels, worked with the sacred, but inoffensive, monogram IHS.

Another well-known funeral pall, which is now kept in the Victoria and Albert Museum, is called the Fayrey Pall, and was formerly in the possession of Dunstable Church. It is said to have been presented to the Fraternity of Saint John the Baptist at Dunstable either by Henry Fayrey, who died in 1516, or by another member of his family at that time. The Fraternity of Saint John the Baptist was a religious and charitable group, which was founded at Dunstable in 1442 and dissolved in 1547. The pall has a centre panel of cloth of gold with a woven pattern of a wavy stem, bearing conventional flowers and leaves in crimson velvet pile with gold loops. The four side panels are of violet velvet, and are embroidered with the figure of Saint John the Baptist preaching. On the two long side panels Saint John is depicted as standing between groups of fourteen men and thirteen women; the first figures in each group are identified by scrolls bearing the names of Henry Fayrey and Agnes Fayrey. There are also shields with coats of arms at each end of these long side panels. On the short side-panels Saint John is shown standing between two kneeling figures, a man and a woman, who are also identified by inscribed scrolls as John Fayrey and Mary Fayrey.

A pall, dating from the early sixteenth century, is the Fishmongers' Pall, which has been considered to be one of the most superb works of its kind, as far as the style of the ornament, the workmanship and the materials used are concerned. It possesses the usual central panel of cloth of gold, with its woven pattern of a wavy stem, bearing leaves and flowers in gold loops and red velvet pile. The two end panels each bear a rich picture, worked in gold and silk, of the patron saint of Fishmongers, Saint Peter seated on a superb throne and crowned with a papal tiara. He holds two keys in one hand and is giving the benediction with the other. On each side of the Saint is a kneeling angel, who is censing him with one hand and holding a golden vase with the other. Each of the long side panels depicts a central building in which Christ is shown delivering the keys to Saint Peter, who kneels before Him, dressed in the same way as he was on the end panels, but with a glory around his head and no crown. Christ is dressed in a crimson-coloured robe with raised

gold work and wears a rich inner vesture of purple; around His head is a jewelled glory. This central picture has the richly emblazoned arms of the Fishmongers on either side of it, supported by a merman and a mermaid: the merman is wearing gold armour, and the mermaid is nude, her body beautifully worked in white silk, with her long tresses in gold thread. There is a fringe of gold and purple silk thread all round the pall.

The Gild of Broderers

The high standard of embroidery, which had been developed in this country in the fourteenth century, and which has never been surpassed at any other time, is thought to have been related to the fact that a 'Gild of Broderers' was in existence here from as far back as the eleventh century. This guild set up rigid rules for the training of apprentices and for the maintenance of high standards of material and technique, but, as we have seen, circumstances occurring in the fifteenth century caused these rules to be relaxed, with a subsequent decline in the standard of the work produced. It seems that it was in what proved to be a vain attempt to restore some of its former glory to English embroidery, as produced in the professional workshops, that the Gild of Broderers was raised in 1561 to the dignity of a chartered body. The attempt failed in its objective as a result of a new Statute of Apprentices, which was initiated in 1563. This statute applied to the whole country and was intended to replace the old guild system, which had only been concerned with the chartered towns and had prevented much of the unemployed rural population from obtaining work in the trading and manufacturing industries by restricting the numbers of people accepted for apprenticeship and by limiting these to the children of the comparatively wealthy. The new statute stated that all craftsmen should be expected to serve an apprenticeship of seven years under a master of their particular craft, who was made personally responsible for them. The effect of this was that many craftsmen, who wished to set up in competition with the guilds, now moved out of the charted towns into the uncharted market towns, where they were free to practice their crafts without being subject to the restricting rules of the guilds. As a result of this change, goods were produced, which were considerably cheaper than they had been before, and this fact attracted many customers away from the chartered towns, but the very high standards, that had been set up by the guilds, were no longer maintained.

The professional workshops still continued to carry out important commissions, such as work for the Livery Companies and other ceremonial embroideries, but they found themselves increasingly up against opposition from amateur embroiderers. They no longer enjoyed Church sponsorship in their work, and the type of embroidery most in demand became ever more secular in nature, with the result that the embroiderers themselves no longer needed to have such expert knowledge of technique. More and more people were thus able to work their own furnishings with the assistance of one professional embroiderer to a group of several amateur workers, who were invariably well-to-do ladies. They certainly appear to have enjoyed themselves in doing this, as we can judge from the many pieces of work which have come down to us, and which, although quite considerable in amount, are only a minute part of the total of works of embroidery, which records show us were produced at that time.

From the wording of a petition, made to King Charles I in 1634, it would appear that the trade of the Broderers was by then 'so much decayed and grown out of use, that a great part of the Company, for want of employment, are so much impoverished that they are constrained to become porters, waterbearers and the like.'[1] The Broderers still preserved right into the nineteenth century the small Hall in Gutter Lane in the City of London, which they had acquired early in the

Altar frontal, English 1535-1555   The velvet background has applied motifs embroidered on linen with silk, silver-gilt and silver threads in split, brick and satin stitches and some couched work. This altar frontal shows Ralph Nevill, fourth Earl of Westmorland, and his seven sons on one side, with Christ on the Cross between the Virgin and Saint John in the centre, and on the other side Lady Catherine Stafford and her 13 daughters. Ralph Nevill and Lady Catherine were married in 1523
Victoria and Albert Museum, London

The Calthorpe Purse, mid sixteenth century   This purse has four shield-shaped side panels exhibiting the coats of arms of the Calthorpe family. It was probably used as an alms-bag or holder for presents of money or jewellery to be given to friends or to royalty at the New Year. It is worked in tent stitch on very fine linen canvas with approximately 1250 stitches to the square inch (centimetre)
Victoria and Albert Museum, London

---

[1] Hazlitt, W C   *The Livery Companies of the City of London*, page 392, 1892.

reign of King Henry VIII, but any connection with the trade of the embroiderer had long since ceased.

The Reformation and the Dissolution of the Monasteries

The year 1485 and the start of the Tudor period in English history is often regarded as the beginning of the modern world, but it did not in reality mark the immediate and sudden end of all things mediaeval in this country. Both King Henry VII and the youthful Henry VIII were good orthodox catholics, and the Church continued more or less as before, although it was incurring increasing unpopularity as a result of events connected with the Reformation in Europe and the influence of the Renaissance, It was not until some fifty years later that Henry VIII, having taken the papal power into his own hands, finally went ahead with the dissolution of the monasteries. With the aid of Parliament he effected a revolution against the Church which, more than any other single event, marked the end of mediaeval society in England, and with it the end of the finest period of embroidery that the Western world has ever known.

As a result of the dissolution of the monasteries much hardship and considerable unemployment ensued. In those days the monasteries were almost like small towns, and they employed a large number of local people as domestic servants. These workers were in many cases more numerous than the monks themselves, so that, although many of the monastic buildings and abbeys were bought by the gentry, who doubtless took on some of the 'serving men' as well, a very large number of these unfortunates were reduced to a life of beggary. The monks fared considerably better, as they were given adequate pensions, and many, who sincerely wished to reform the Catholic Church, and who felt able to adapt their religious views in accor-dance with the changes occurring at this time, found employment as clergymen, and some even as bishops in the new Church.[1]

Church embroideries continued to be produced, but with a difference: they no longer glorified the Church of Rome, and all references to the Virgin Mary were forbidden. This had a disastrous effect on the glorious vestments and Church ornaments in general: many of the old copes and chasubles were sold to wealthy City merchants, who hurriedly obliterated the offending symbols by having them cut out and replaced by more acceptable Protestant ones; some were sold to foreigners, while others were merely smuggled abroad; and a large number quietly disappeared into the homes of wealthy Catholics, where they lay hidden for many, many years, or were cut up and altered, so that they could be used for secular purposes. The cruellest fate of all was reserved for some of the most richly embroidered vestments, which were simply destroyed by burning in order that the precious gold, which had been used in working them, might be recovered.

Although in this way the great mediaeval tradition of English embroidery virtually came to an end, there was no actual reduction in the amount of needlework being produced at the time. The reappearance in the outer world of some two thousand nuns, all members of well-to-do families and most of them with a very sound knowledge of embroidery, must have done much to improve the general standard of secular work. As a result a very different type of embroidery now emerged, that was quickly to develop and reach a new high peak of technical perfection in the reign of Queen Elizabeth I.

---

[1] Trevelyan, G M *English Social History*, page 109, 1944.

The Elizabethan period

Conditions having greatly improved in the country with the establishment of a middle class at the expense of the Church, more people other than the nobility were beginning to look for greater luxury in the home. The wealth and power of the country gentleman had been greatly increased, partly by the acquisition of monastic land at a very economical price, and partly by his becoming involved in the wool and the cloth trade and in overseas commerce. Many of the old monastery buildings were altered and adapted to a more comfortable style of living, whilst the large and small Tudor houses, many of which are still to be seen in the English countryside to this day,

were being built with the new bricks. People took immense pride in the ownership of these houses and filled them with many beautiful things.

Gardens also became exceedingly popular at this time. Parks were laid out around the large country houses and many new specimens of tree were introduced, among which herds of deer wandered. The gentry also became conscious of

Bed valances of the late sixteenth century, depicting the story of Cinyras and Myrrha and Venus and Adonis. They are worked on linen canvas with coloured wools and silks in tent stitch and with a small amount of raised work
Victoria and Albert Museum, London

Detail of a French sixteenth century woven tapestry
The designs of many English canvas work panels were greatly influenced by those of the woven tapestries of France

showing clouds and outsize birds. Every inch of the canvas is filled with a variety of objects: human figures, birds, animals, flowers, trees, fountains, buildings, arches and covered walks.

It became popular during the late sixteenth century for sets of three such canvas work panels to be made up as valances for the tops of the four-poster beds, that were then being used. One can gaze upon these valances for a long time and still find something fresh to observe, all of which causes one to marvel at the time and patience that must have been expended, and the skill that was needed to produce such unique pieces of work. The designs were probably based on French and Flemish engravings of the period, and they also appear to have been influenced in the actual working by the French Gothic tapestries. It does not seem that slavish copies of the engravings were made, but, whether this was the case or not, the designs have been most skilfully adapted for working on canvas. The tapesty technique of shading by means of hatchings has been cleverly imitated on canvas in the working of the little hillocks, which appear in such scenes, and the conventional treatment of trees, which occurs in the working of tapestries, as well as the general habit of sprinkling a growth of flowers and a large number of animals everywhere, have also been adopted.

It is not always fully realized what a large number of hours of work would be necessary for the preparation and production of these large pieces of Elizabethan canvas work. A full-sized drawing, perfect in every detail, would first have to be made by the designer. This would then be outlined in black paint with a fine brush, in order that the apprentices could see it well enough to trace the design on to the canvas. For this to be done the outlined design would be placed behind the canvas, which would already have been mounted on a wooden frame, and it would be firmly pinned to the canvas. The frame would then be ready to be propped up in a position in which the light could clearly show up the design and enable the tracers to trace it through on to the canvas. It would be laboriously traced with black or sepia paint on to the canvas, using a fine paint brush. Two or more apprentices would have been employed on this task, according to the size of the panel, and only after several days of labour would the canvas finally have been ready to be worked.

It should be noted here that the canvas, which was used for this kind of embroidery during the Elizabethan period, was a type of linen canvas

the flower garden and vied with one another in possessing the latest imports of foreign plants, which included not only flowers of many kinds, but also vegetables. These gardens became places in which the well-to-do Elizabethans enjoyed making music and dancing during the summer months. They also made a fine setting for the innumerable masques and revels which were so popular in those days.

A record of the beauty of these Elizabethan gardens may still be seen in the large bed hangings, valences, table carpets and chair and bench coverings, which were made at the time and still survive to show us the pergolas, fountains and streams, the mazes and the herb and knot gardens with their box hedges, all of which were so dear to their Elizabethan owners. This was the period of our history when canvas work, as we know it today, really came into its own. Suddenly the large wall hangings, table carpets and bed hangings appeared on the scene, all worked on canvas in tent stitch. Using this medium, figures of people, dressed in contemporary costume, are shown enacting scenes, which were based on classical, and sometimes on religious themes. They were also occasionally depicted in scenes of everyday life in Tudor times. The figures appear disporting themselves against a background of an Elizabethan garden, which recedes into a narrow strip of sky,

Long cushion cover of the mid sixteenth century This cushion bears the arms attributed to John Warneford of Sevenhampton in Wiltshire and his wife, Susanna Yates. It is worked with coloured silks in tent stitch on linen canvas *Victoria and Albert Museum, London*

which had a mesh of from 16 to 20 threads to the inch (25 mm). It was a much coarser and more open material than had been used previously, and it shows, in fact, the early beginning of the kind of canvas we use for our embroidery today. In previous years, when the linen background was a very much finer and more closely woven fabric, the designs would have been pricked all round with a needle, before being placed on top of the linen. A powder, such as powdered charcoal, would then have been rubbed all over the design and would have penetrated the pricked holes, so that, when the design was removed, a fine dotted line of powder remained on the background fabric as a guide for the tracer to paint in with a fine paint brush and black water-colour, or some other medium. This prick-and-pounce method, as it is called, is the traditional way of transferring an original design on to a closely woven fabric, but it would not be possible to use this method to transfer a design on to an open-mesh canvas.

When the process of tracing the design on to the canvas had been completed, several embroiderers, working side by side along the two long sides of the frame, would begin their task. The silks and wools, that would be needed for the work, would already have been dyed, and each worker would be given an allocation of materials with which to embroider a specific area. A coloured cartoon would also have been supplied to give the embroiderers a guide to the colours they would have to use and the positions in which they should use them. The actual embroidering of these large Tudor panels was all done in tent stitch. This is one of the smallest stitches that can be used on canvas. It is worked at an angle across one intersection of the canvas, with all the individual stitches sloping in the same direction.

It can thus be seen that it was no light matter to undertake a task of this magnitude, and it would probably have been far beyond the capabilities of a small group of amateurs to attempt such a piece of work. We must, therefore, assume that most, if not all, of the large pieces of canvas embroidery of the Elizabethan period were still being done by highly skilled professionals, operating in workshops with several people working together on one large frame.

Table carpets

Another way, in which the new middle classes during the sixteenth century sought to beautify their homes, was in the production of what are called table carpets, and these were also worked

Detail of the Gifford Table Carpet, mid sixteenth century
This is a detail of the centre of the table carpet with the arms of Gifford within a wreath of flowers. It is worked on linen canvas with coloured wools in tent stitch
Victoria and Albert Museum, London

in canvas embroidery. The word carpet or 'carpett', as it is spelt in the old inventories, was used to distinguish a table cover from a covering for the floor, which was called a 'tapet'. It had been the practice from earlier days in the homes of the upper classes to have covers made to place over the plain wooden trestle tables, that were then in use, and, with the revival of English embroidery in the Tudor period, magnificient carpets were worked on canvas to be used for this purpose. Some such household articles were also woven at this time, as the earliest known table carpet of Tudor times is, in fact, a tapestry. Known as the Luttrell Table Carpet, it is thought to date from about 1520, and to have been woven in Flanders to an English design. The earliest known example of a canvas work table carpet is the Gifford Table Carpet, the date of which is estimated to have been about 1550.

The Gifford Table Carpet, which is now in the Victoria Albert Museum, measures 18 ft x 4 ft 8 in. (5.5 m x 1.4 m) and is worked in wool in tent stitch on a very fine linen canvas of approximately 20 threads to the inch (25 mm). The design consists of a long central panel, worked in a small, geometric, diaper pattern, which is itself surrounded by a border, based on another geometric pattern. There are three medallions set in the central panel, and the middle one of these contains what is probably the coat of arms of the Gifford

Bradford Table Carpet, English, late sixteenth century
This table carpet, which is 13 ft long x 5 ft 9 in. wide (3.9 m x 1.7 m), is worked with silk in tent stitch on linen canvas *Victoria and Albert Museum, London*

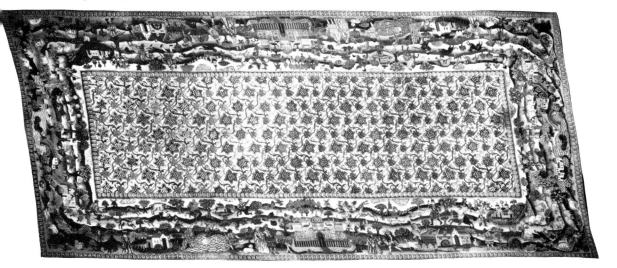

Bradford Table Carpet   Detail A shows the shepherd with his crook rounding up his flock
Victoria and Albert Museum, London

Bradford Table Carpet   Detail B shows a well fenced-in country house with a fine display of black smoke issuing from the chimney
Victoria and Albert Museum, London

family, having a shield bearing three lions passant with a crest above it, showing a hand holding up the antlers of a stag. The other two medallions show a stag standing under an oak tree. Each of the three medallions is encircled by a wreath of flowers in which are depicted the Tudor rose, pinks and acorns.

The Bradford Table Carpet is thought to date from the late sixteenth century. This well-known table carpet, which is also to be seen in the Victoria and Albert Museum in London, is worked in coloured silks in tent stitch on a fine linen canvas of approximately 20 threads to the inch (25 mm). The design has a wide border, depicting Elizabethan life, surrounding a central panel, which has an all-over pattern of a trellis covered with vine leaves and bunches of grapes. The border design, which is the most interesting part of the carpet, shows the new type of manor house of this period, with its owners all splendidly clothed, enjoying the country air. The village is also shown in the background, with the village people pursuing their individual occupations: there are the fisherman, the huntsman with his horn and the shepherd with his crook; there are dogs, horses and sheep, and the ubiquitous hare — all are depicted there. The design is what is commonly known as a 'half-design', which means that the draughtsman only drew it up for the length of one long side and one short side of the border, and to complete the whole piece the same 'half-design' was repeated along the other long and short sides of the border. It is noticeable, when one examines the worked carpet, that at one joining point of the two halves of the design no attempt has been made to effect the simple adjustment, which is necessary to make sure the earth shapes flow easily together. The person who embroidered this part of the panel obviously had no great knowledge of drawing and just embroidered the shapes as they appeared to him or her, without regard for the whole border design.

The over-all shape of this particular table carpet has unfortunately become distorted in the working, so that it almost appears not to have been worked on a frame, something which is, however, very unlikely to have been the case. The distortion is undoubtedly due to two things, which are unfortunately only too common in canvas work. Firstly, there is the very nature of the stitch which has been used here: this is tent stitch, the basic stitch of canvas embroidery, which, as has already been mentioned, is a diagonal stitch, worked over one intersection of the canvas, and which has a

Bradford Table Carpet Detail C shows the huntsman blowing his horn and accompanied by his spotted dog
Victoria and Albert Museum, London

tendency to pull the embroidery out of the straight, even when a smaller piece is being worked upon a frame. It is difficult sometimes to correct this tendency today, when using a coarser canvas, so that with a large panel, such as the one in question with its fine, pliable canvas, it could well have been impossible to do so. The second reason for the distortion is the fact that this table carpet has been worked entirely in silk. It might have been possible to rectify the distortion, if it had been worked in wool, with only a small amount of silk, but silk, unlike wool, has no elasticity and consequently exerts a very strong pulling effect on the canvas, always pulling it in the direction of the tent stitch along the diagonal. The tension thus created is such, that it would be exceedingly unwise to attempt to straighten the work out.

This distortion, which appears not only on the Bradford Table Carpet, but also on many other pieces of canvas work of this period, does show us that the most suitable fibre for working on canvas is wool, with only a little silk used for rendering high lights. It is, in fact, noticeable that there was a change during the later part of the Elizabethan period from the exclusive use of silk on canvas to the working of such large panels mainly in wool, with only a small amount of silk.

Turkey work

A special type of canvas work, which appeared in England in the sixteenth century, was Turkey work. No one knows with any certainty exactly when it was first introduced into this country, but

43

A sketch of fragments of a table carpet of the late sixteenth century, worked on linen canvas with coloured wools and silk in tent, cross and long-legged cross stitches *Victoria and Albert Museum, London*

it is generally assumed that it must have been in the early years of the sixteenth century, as Cardinal Wolsey is reputed to have had the first woven carpets of this kind brought from Turkey to furnish his new palace at Hampton Court in the 1520s, and it is thought probable that English Turkey work was the result of an attempt at that time to imitate on coarse canvas the technique of these woven carpets. The first examples of work of this kind on canvas may, however, have been produced even earlier than this, as in an inventory of goods belonging to Lord Admiral Seymour, made at the

Sketch detail of an English Turkey-work carpet, dated 1600   The actual carpet is in the *Victoria and Albert Museum, London*

time of his attainder in 1549, mention is made of old Turkey work cupboard cloths and old Turkey work carpets. As this type of work is reasonably hard-wearing, one would expect that the cupboard cloths at least would have a very considerable life span, so that the pieces mentioned here could have been produced earlier than the sixteenth century. There is, however, no means of knowing for sure, whether these early examples of Turkey work were done on canvas or were woven carpets, which had been imported from Turkey.

English Turkey work is done with coarse wool on a tough, coarse linen canvas. Rows of Ghiordes knots (also called Turkey Rug knots) are worked from left to right across the area of canvas to be covered, and the wool is clipped short on the front of the work to form a close pile, similar to that of the woven Turkey carpets. It was widely used for such things as cushions, bench covers and chair seats, as well as for the so-called 'foot carpets' of the period. The designs employed in the work were usually heraldic designs or all-over floral patterns, worked in many colours and having only small areas of undecorated background. It remained popular right up to about the beginning of the eighteenth century, when it seems finally to have gone out of fashion, although even in the twenties and thirties of the present century Turkey work chair seats and stair-treads were still being produced on coarse canvas, but only as reproductions of the seventeenth century type of work.

There is an interesting account of the wife of Philip Howard, the Earl of Arundel (1557-1595), who appeared to know exactly what she wanted and would permit no one residing in her house to remain idle for more than a short time. As was usual in those days, the Countess employed an embroiderer, and this particular person was especially skilled in Turkey work, or 'cut work', as it was sometimes called. Any guests, finding themselves with nothing to do, would be firmly dispatched to aid the embroiderer in her work. It was not only guests and women of the household, however, who were pressed into helping in this way, but occasionally the assistance of a number of outside embroiderers was also sought, when the completion of a particular piece was urgently required. These outside helpers were paid, we learn, the sum of eight pence a day for their labour.[1]

[1] Jourdain, M *The History of English Secular Embroidery*, London, 1910.

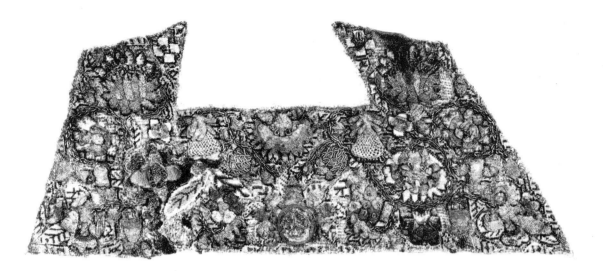

Panel of embroidery of the late sixteenth century   This panel, 5 in. x 11½ in. (12.7 cm x 29.2 cm), is worked on linen canvas in tent stitch, with couched threads and some raised work
Victoria and Albert Museum, London

Book covers

In addition to large panels of canvas work and examples of English Turkey work, the Tudor period also saw the production of numerous small pieces of canvas embroidery. Many of these were in the form of book covers, purses and bags for special purposes, such as for carrying books of prayers or for the protection of seals on important documents. The sixteenth century examples of this kind of work were done on canvas, but sometimes the main motifs of a design were then cut out and applied on to velvet, a practice which was not followed in the seventeenth century.

Most of these book covers were made for use on religious books, such as Bibles and Books of Prayers. Generally they were worked in tent stitch with silk thread on a canvas which had been woven with approximately 18 to 20 threads to one inch (25 mm), and the embroiderers who worked them were largely amateurs.

Two such small books, which survive to this day, had manuscripts written by the young Princess Elizabeth at the age of eleven and twelve respectively, and their embroidered covers were also worked by her on canvas. The first one is entitled *The Miroir or Glasse of the Synneful Soul* and was written in 1544, and the other is *The Prayers of Queen Katherine Parr*, and was produced a year later. The design for the cover of the first of these books shows in the centre of the front cover the Queen's initials, KP, enclosed by interlaced strap-

Embroidered book-binding   on a small volume, entitled *The Miroir or Glasse of the Synneful Soul*, which was translated by the Princess Elizabeth — afterwards Queen Elizabeth I — 'out of Frenche ryme into English prose, joyning the sentences together as well as the capacitie of my symple witte and small lerning coulde extende themselves'. The embroidered binding is also believed to have been worked by Elizabeth, and the initials, K P, suggest that it was intended as a present for her step-mother, Queen Katharine Parr. The book is dedicated 'From Assherige, the last daye of the yeare of our Lord God 1544'. Plaited gold and silver thread has been used for the interlacing around the initials *Bodleian Library, Oxford*

work, which is worked in braid stitch in gold and silver, with the flower of a heartsease, which is reputed to have been Elizabeth's favourite flower, worked in high relief in each corner. The canvas ground is worked in blue silk in a stitch, which we know today as encroaching Gobelin stitch, worked horizontally across the canvas.

The second book, which Elizabeth dedicated to her father, King Henry VIII, followed similar lines to the first in the details of its cover design, but he monogram of the Queen is larger and more complex, and it has two smaller Hs placed one above and one below the Queen's initials, with elaborate interlacing of braid stitch surrounding it. This large monogram is worked in blue silk and silver thread, with the smaller Hs in gold thread and red silk. The heartsease flowers, worked in yellow and purple silk, are once again placed in the corners. The background is worked in red silk. This second book contains the prayers and meditations of Queen Katherine Parr, which she wrote originally in English, but which Princess Elizabeth at the age of twelve translated into Latin, French and Italian.

It is recorded by Bishop Montague in 1611, that Mary, Queen of Scots, also wrote in 1579 a book of verse in French for her son, and that she embroidered the cover 'with a needle'. It is impossible to say if this book cover was embroidered on canvas or not, as it has now unfortunately disappeared.

Many of these embroidered book covers, which are still in existence, are very small in size, and they are excellent examples of the skill of their makers. They were generally finished off with ties of silk attached to them, and, as often happened later in the seventeenth century, cases and extra covers were made to protect the embroidered bindings themselves. These outer covers were also adorned with embroidery and were sometimes made in the form of a bag with draw-strings, elaborately ornamented with tassels of silk.

Embroidered book covers appear to have been a peculiarly English product. The Dutch possess the best of the continental examples of this type of embroidered article, while the French and Italians appear to have had little or no interest in such things. Very special books are still covered with embroidery today, but it is mostly worked on silk material with silk and metal thread, and only occasionally on canvas, which is rather surprising, when one considers the long-lasting qualities of fine canvas, which is clearly an ideal material for the purpose.

Mary, Queen of Scots (1542-1587)

The romantic history surrounding Mary, Queen of Scots, is such that there is a tendency to imagine that she was responsible for the working of a very large amount of embroidery, far more, in fact, than she or any other human being could have achieved in her life-time with its many vicissitudes. It is, however, safe to say that she was a keen needlewoman, who, it has been suggested, had benefited in her youth in France from the instruction she received from Catherine de Medici, her mother-in-law, who was herself reputed to have been a needlewoman of great ability. Examples of Mary's work on canvas, which have survived to the present time, do not, in point of fact, bear out this suggestion that she had learnt her craft in France, as they show no evidence of French influence, but are completely English in style.

It was during the time when she was imprisoned in Lochleven Castle that Mary was thought to have worked a number of large pieces of embroidery, which have continued to be attributed to her over the years in Scotland. According to the records, however, it does not seem that she was allowed enough materials to have been able to achieve this amount of work during the short period of less than a year that she remained at Lochleven. It is reported that she only received a few small parcels at this time, containing a minute quantity of silk and a few hanks of gold and silver thread. One parcel is mentioned, which contained a small piece of canvas on which a design with eighteen small flowers was painted. The outlines were already worked in black silk, and there were in the parcel just a few hanks of assorted coloured silks with which Mary could complete the working of the canvas. This is said to have been the meagre ration of materials, which she received whilst at Lochleven, and it would certainly not have enabled her to work the large hangings which have been accredited to her, especially as they are mainly worked in wool with only a little silk, and the pieces of embroidery, that we can safely assume to have been hers, are all worked in silk with some gold and silver thread.

When Mary escaped into England in 1568 after this period of captivity in Scotland, it was fortunate for her that she was eventually placed by Queen Elizabeth I in the custody of the Earl of Shrewsbury, whose wife, the famous Bess of Hardwick, was also a skilled needlewoman. The many years of captivity that followed for Mary in England certainly gave her plenty of opportunity to work on her embroideries. She was moved from house to house in the various places owned by the Earl of Shrewsbury. First, we know, she was at Tutbury in Staffordshire; then in Sheffield Castle, where she remained for thirteen years, until in 1586 she was moved again, and this time to Chartley, which was also in Staffordshire; finally she went to Fotheringay, where she was tried and executed.

Mary and Bess had a common interest in embroidery, and they worked together on the now famous Oxburgh Panels. There is a letter from Lord Shrewsbury to Lord William Cecil which contains the following statement: 'The Queen daily resorts to my wife's chamber, where with Lady Leviston and Mrs Seton she sits working with her 'nydill' '. To what extent Mary was also involved in the working of the fine collection of needlework wall-hangings and embroidered furniture covers, which are to be seen at Hardwick Hall in Derbyshire, is not certain. It is really only safe to credit her personally with those pieces on which she worked her monogram, often surmounted with a crown. We known that she was never held captive in the present Hardwick Hall, as that was a new building, erected after her execution, and the embroideries must have been taken there at a later date.

The Oxburgh Panels consists of thirty-seven small medallions, worked on linen canvas with silk in tent stitch and cross stitch. The canvas used was of fine linen thread in tabby weave, a material which was often woven in the households of wealthy embroiderers. It was a single mesh canvas, which was very similar to that used today, but was very much more pliable. There has been a suggestion that the canvas used for the Oxburgh Panels was a double mesh canvas, but, if the worn parts are examined, it can be clearly seen that the double mesh effect is caused by the working of cross stitch, which has permanently distorted the canvas and thus given it the appearance of being double-mesh. Other worn parts on the same panel, which are worked in tent stitch, reveal the true nature of the canvas. It was not until many years later in the Victorian era that double-thread canvas was introduced. Mary and Bess each signed the pieces they embroidered with their own ciphers, and the unsigned medallions were, no doubt, worked by other ladies of the household or by the professional embroiderers, three of whom are

Oxburgh Hanging, 1570 See also colour plate 4 *Detail A* An elephant. The design was taken from an illustration in Konrad Gesner's *Icones Animalium*, printed in Zürich in 1560 *Victoria and Albert Museum, London*

Oxburgh Hanging, 1570 *Detail B* Knotted serpentes *Victoria and Albert Museum, London*

known to have worked with Mary at one period in her years of imprisonment. The embroidered medallions, when finished, were applied to a dark green velvet background.

When one examines Mary's canvas work on the Oxburgh Panel, one is forced to the conclusion that her greatest interest must have been in the design and its subject matter, rather than in the actual working, which is often rough and badly

Oxburgh Hanging, 1570 *Detail C* This shows Mary's own cipher and a giant sun, which is shining down on to some marigolds, the flower which Mary later adopted as her particular emblem
Victoria and Albert Museum, London

Cushion cover of the sixteenth century This piece was worked by Mary, Queen of Scots, with silk in tent stitch, and using cross stitch, worked over one intersection of the canvas, for the background. The thistle, the lily and the rose, which stand for Scotland, France and England, are shown in the spaces between an entwined fret of braid stitch. The centre panel shows two frogs at a well-head, a scene which probably implies a cryptic message of the type so beloved by Mary *Hardwick Hall, National Trust*

finished. When it is realised that a professional draughtsman probably drew the design and traced it on to the canvas, and in addition worked all the outlines of the design, when traced, in order to retain the accuracy of the original drawing, one can see that it would only require a rudimentary knowledge of canvas work in the embroiderer to be able to complete a given piece successfully. Parts of the exposed canvas show the method that was employed in drawing the design on to the canvas, and also how it was indicated to the workers which parts were to be shaded by painting in areas in sepia colour. It is interesting to see the enormous amount of help which was given to the amateur embroiderers in those days and to realise that some form of assistance in the production of designs suitable for embroidery appears to have gone on throughout the centuries, even down to our own days with the preparation of painted canvases.

Sketch from The Heroicall Devises of M Claudius Paradin
1   The peacock-feather fan and the flies (Tolle voluptatis stimulos. Take awaie the prickles of pleasure.)
2   The snake in the strawberry plant. (Latet anguis in herba. The adder lurketh priuilie in the grasse.) This sketch shows examples of the type of device which interested Mary, Queen of Scots

Elizabethan Long Cushion (detail)   The whole cushion is 3 ft 5 in. long x 1 ft 10½ in. wide (104 cm x 52 cm) and is worked in tent stitch with a certain amount of cross stitch and couching, using silk and silver thread on linen canvas. The various elements of the design have then been cut out and applied to a ground of white satin
Victoria and Albert Museum, London

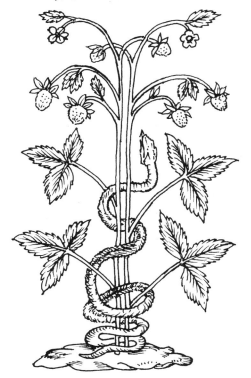

49

A painted detail of a square cushion-cover of the late sixteenth century The original cushion-cover is worked with wool and silk on linen canvas in cross and long-legged cross stitches. The motif, which is depicted here, is repeated diagonally to form the complete design for the cushion cover, which is 19½ in. long x 19 in. wide (49 cm x 45 cm). The colours of the wools used are dark blue-green, light green, yellow, pink, carmine and light magenta. The silks are in light shades of blue, yellow, brown and cream

Mary's own medallions on the Oxburgh Panel are worked on a canvas with 18 threads to the inch (25 mm). They are worked almost entirely in tent stitch and cross stitch with a rich, heavy, lightly spun floss silk. It is probably the high quality of this long-staple silk which accounts for the reasonably good condition of the panel today.

The Queen of Scots' great interest appears to have been the new and exciting pastime of solving the meanings of various emblematic devices, which were appearing in books at that time. Originating in Italy, they soon appeared in France, and Mary would have had no difficulty in obtaining them. Many of the emblems used by her in working her share of the Oxburgh Panels were exact copies of designs taken from the most popular pattern book of the day, *Devises Héroiques* by Claude Paradin, which was published in Lyons in the year 1557. The book was well illustrated with very workable suggestions for designs which could be embroidered on canvas. It was the age of riddles, symbolism, anagrams and puns, so it is not surprising to find its fresh and new ideas reflected in the embroidery of the period. The emblems with their Latin mottoes, used by Mary, Queen of Scots, were devices which illustrated an idea, and which often held a double meaning. These ideas were naturally more easily understood and more fully appreciated at that time, than they are today, when the significance of many of the emblems is no longer apparent to us.

Needles

The needle is the one important implement which is essential to the working of embroidery and yet it is rarely mentioned in the history of this craft. It has, however, often been suggested that the sudden flowering of canvas work, and the tremendous increase in the amount that was produced in the sixteenth century, was the result of the introduction into England at that time of the steel needle, a suggestion which nevertheless overlooks the fact that highly perfected needles must have been used here before that date and especially for the working of the very fine pieces of the *Opus Anglicanum* in the thirteenth and fourteenth centuries.

The Chinese knew all about the making of steel needles many centuries before Christ, and the knowledge of how such things were made reached India and the Near East during the time of the Pharoahs. Damascus was long-famed for the skill of its people in metalwork, and it became an important centre for the making of fine needles during the period of the Roman Empire. The steel needles, which were then produced, were without doubt of comparable quality with our modern, machine-made ones. French inventories of the fourteenth century mention 'Aiguilles d'Antioche' (needles from Antioch) and suggest that they were very valuable objects, possessed only by the very wealthy members of society.

During the Middle Ages in England the monasteries were involved in the making of needles, but these seem to have been of a pretty primitive type and were probably made of bronze. They were generally alluded to as packing needles and would have been used for stitching up the rough kind of material with which all merchandise was covered as it travelled around the countryside. It is interesting to note that a derelict needle mill remained on the site of Bordesley Abbey long after the dissolution of the monasteries in the reign of King Henry VIII, and that the important needlemaking centre of

modern times at Redditch in Worcestershire is situated in the same part of the country.[1]

Later in the sixteenth century there was a definite influx into England of good steel needles, which came mainly from Spain, being produced in Cordoba, which became at that time the most important centre for the making of needles in Western Europe. During the reign of Mary Tudor it is reported that some needles were made in the city of London by a negro (now thought to have been a Moor from Spain), but that he kept the secrets of his trade to himself, so that, when he died, his craft died with him, and it was not until the eighth year of the reign of Queen Elizabeth I that 'the art of making Spanish needles was first taught in England by Elias Crouse (or Krause), a German.'[2]

There is no doubt that good needles were much easier to obtain in the reign of Elizabeth I than they had been earlier, and for many years increasing numbers of people were able to avail themselves of a supply of 'Spanish needles' for doing embroidery. They were cheaper to buy than the earlier needles had been, were of a higher quality

Long cushion cover of the late sixteenth century This is worked on linen canvas with coloured silks and silver and silver-gilt threads in tent, cross, long-legged cross and stem stitches and with laid work, applied on to black velvet *Victoria and Albert Museum, London*

Sketch of a tent and cross stitch 'slip', worked on canvas and applied to the centre of the long velvet cushion cover shown above

[1] Andere, Mary *Old Needlework Boxes and Tools*, David and Charles 1971.

[2] Stow, John *Annales or a General Chronicle of England*, 1631.

51

and stronger than before and were, therefore, more suitable for working on the coarser canvas used in the newer type of canvas work. They did not, however, have any noticeable effect on the standard of embroidery as a whole, which is more likely to have been influenced by the greater availability of the new printed books, such as herbals and beastiaries with their illustrations of flowers and animals, which could easily be copied. These latter encouraged not only members of the nobility, but also embroiderers of the new middle class to work furnishings for their homes.

An Italian **valance** or border of the late sixteenth century, worked in long satin stitches with coloured floss silks on black canvas

52

The seventeenth century

The type of canvas work, which had become popular during the reign of Queen Elizabeth I, continued into the reign of King James I, and such things as bed hangings and valances were embroidered in much the same way during the early years of the seventeenth century as they had been during the later years of the sixteenth. Some of the designs used do, however, show a gradual change of style, and this can be seen, for example, in the curtains and valances around the bed in the Great Chamber at Parham House in West Sussex, which were worked about the year 1615, and which constitute a supreme example of the use of *point d'hongrie* in working on canvas with silk and wool. It should be noted, that this highly valued, early example of the use of *point d'hongrie* in working on canvas in this country did not form part of a general change, and that it was not until the eighteenth century that this type of work became really popular.

Another change, which gradually developed in the type of canvas work, which was produced in the reign of James I, was the tendency towards the working of smaller pieces than before. This resulted in part from the use of wood panelling, which became the vogue in the homes of the early seventeenth century, and which, by breaking up

Bed curtains and valences of the early seventeenth century This is a supreme example of the use of point d'hongrie in the working on canvas with silk and wool of four bed curtains, three top valances and three mattress valances. The canvas used was of a narrow width (approx. 9½ in. 24 cm, and this entailed much joining. The colouring is soft and gentle, being in shades of pink, a warm brown, yellow and green, colours which blend to give a delightful effect *Parham Park, Sussex*

A late seventeenth century Italian border, worked on canvas in point d'hongrie stitch with wool, and with a yellow silk background

the wall space into smaller areas, gave an impetus to the fashion for small, framed pictures to replace the very large, tent stitch panels of the Elizabethan age. The panelled walls of the smaller rooms of the time were highly suitable for displaying these small pictures, which were still worked in tent stitch, but on a very much finer canvas than before — often it was as fine as 30 threads or more to the inch (25 mm). Another reason for the tendency towards the working of smaller pieces of canvas embroidery during the seventeenth century was the fact that this type of work was moving more and more into the hands of amateur embroiderers, whereas the large pieces of the Elizabethan period had been done mainly by professional workers, who had only a few amateurs associated with them.

Both mythological and biblical figures are depicted in these smaller Jacobean canvas work pictures. They are all attired in contemporary costume, and the action depicted is taking place in modern surroundings, with many of the designs clearly based on Flemish originals. The picture books of the previous century with wood cuts and engravings illustrating biblical themes, as well as stories from the works of classical writers, such as

Small canvas-work picture, English, seventeenth century Elijah and the Widow of Zarephath (I Kings 17) are here depicted, worked with silk and a small amount of wool in tent and rococo stitches. This subject was a great favourite with the canvas workers of the seventeenth century, and this piece may be compared with the sketch of the same subject, which follows
Victoria and Albert Museum, London

the Metamorphoses of the Latin poet Ovid, continued to be very popular. There was a renewed interest in the literature of Greece and Rome at a time when the Bible had just been translated into many European languages, but, as there were in those days numerous people unable to read in any language, further illustrated books, both large and small, based on classical and biblical stories, were published to assist them, and it was these same illustrated books which gave people access to ideas for designs that could be used in their embroidery.

With the size of individual pieces tending to decrease, the designs which were used to work them became simpler and far less extravagant than those of the highly detailed panels of the previous century. Little or no regard was paid to proportion and perspective, and animals, birds, caterpillars and flowers were all used indiscriminately merely to fill an empty space on the canvas of whatever size. There is also a great similarity in the choice of subjects which are depicted on many of the

Seventeenth century canvas-work panel   This panel is worked mainly in tent stitch with some rococo and buttonhole filling stitches in the flower centres. The natural-coloured background is in Hungarian stitch, worked with the stitches lying horizontally across the canvas. The design shows a very prim-faced leopard and a startled lion with a bird above them. The bird's feet are actually there, worked in tent stitch, although they are almost invisible in the photograph
Cecil Higgins Art Gallery, Bedford

Solomon and the Queen of Sheba, English, mid-seventeenth century   A tent-stitch picture, worked with silk on linen canvas
Victoria and Albert Museum, London

seventeenth century embroidered pictures which have survived to the present day. Scenes from the Old Testament story seem to have been the most popular, and some of them were constantly repeated: David and Bathsheba; Solomon and the Queen of Sheba; Jonah and the Whale; Abraham about to sacrifice Isaac; The Judgement of Solomon; Abraham and the Angels and Tobias and the Angel. All of these subjects became so popular that they are seen not only in many pictures, but also on books covers, small cushions and caskets over and over again. These little biblical scenes with figures clad in contemporary costumes are shown taking place in the country-side, which more often than not contains a mansion.

A glorious sun shines out over the scene — and occasionally also the moon — upon the peaceful landscape, where the lion and the leopard, the hare, the dog and the squirrel all sit side by side with their human companions in dreamlike tranquility among the trees and the great flowers.

The preference for depicting biblical scenes, which were taken almost exclusively from the Old Testament, arose from a desire to avoid showing the figure of Christ, the Virgin Mary or the Saints. The Reformation in England had the effect of cutting off all connection with so-called Popish practices and resulted in the avoidance particularly of any reference to the Virgin or the catholic Saints, images of whom had previously occupied a very important place in Church art.

Book covers, bags and purses

The working of embroidered book-covers, bags

Bible cover, dated 1640 The design is worked on canvas in tent stitch, using wool and silk, and the background is in gros point, worked with silver thread. This front cover shows the figure of Faith

On the back cover of this Bible the figure of a woman representing Hope is shown standing beside a large anchor *The Bible Society, London*

and purses, which we have already noticed in the time of Elizabeth I, continued in the Stuart period. The publication of the English translation of the Bible in 1611, the Authorised version, coming at the same time as the Bible was also being translated from Latin into the mother tongues of various other countries in Europe, brought bibles into the hands of the common people, and many seventeenth century embroidered bible-covers are still in existence. They are often quite small and are worked in tent stitch without any heavy raised or padded work, so that many of them are still in a very good condition. One such bible, dated 1640, which is in the library of the Bible Society in London, has a cover worked in tent stitch on canvas. The front cover shows the figure of a woman, representing Faith, who is holding in her hand a plain ribbon, on which the word Faith was probably worked originally, but has been worn off in the course of the years. On the back cover another woman, representing Hope, is depicted standing beside a large anchor. The spine of the book is divided into four sections, as was the common practice then, and these contain the representation of a lily in the top section, a small bird in the next section, a tulip in the third — this was a new import from Holland at that time — and in the final section a seated leopard. Coloured silks have been used to work the design, while silver thread has been used for the background. It is in very good condtion and has obviously been treasured over the centuries. A written note inside this bible states that the cover was worked by the mother of Mrs Mary Bradley, afterwards Mrs Arbuthnot, who lived from 1654 to 1707.

Another book-cover in the same library is that on a Book of Common Prayer, dated 1633. This is a very tiny book, which measures only 2 in. x 4½ in. (5 cm x 11 cm) and is 2½ in (6 cm) thick. It is covered with a coarse canvas, which is lightly worked with silk of a natural colour in an open all-over diaper pattern with tiny rosettes worked in silver. Many of the canvas work book covers of this period were of similar small dimensions.

Yet another excellent example of the book bindings of the seventeenth century, which is worked in tent stitch on canvas, is one produced by Elizabeth Illingworthe in 1613. This shows on the front cover Abraham about to sacrifice Isaac, and on the back a scene depicting Jonah and the Whale. This binding is the work of an amateur, as it is signed quite boldly with her initials and the date when it was worked. People were only now beginning to work their initials on their pieces of

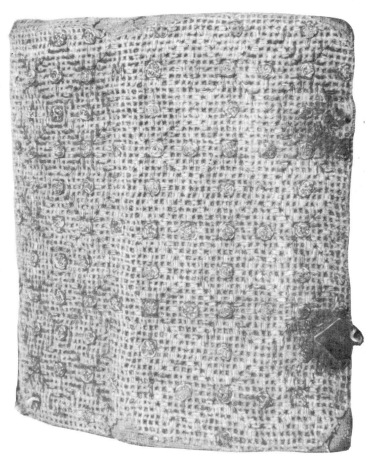

Small Book of Common Prayer. This book is dated 1633 and measures only 4½ in. x 2 in. and is 2½ in. thick (11.4 cm x 5 cm x 6.3 cm). The cover is worked on coarse canvas with a light covering of silk forming an open, all-over, diaper pattern, and with small rosettes executed in silver *The Bible Society, London*

embroidery, but soon it became the custom to sign their full names. This came about when young children were being taught to work samplers, and they not only worked their full names, but also their ages.

Cushion covers

In the reign of King James I many long cushions and other furnishings of a similar nature, worked on canvas, continued to be made in the Elizabethan tradition. From quite early days cushions had been made for a variety of purposes. The seating for ordinary persons often consisted merely of a stone

Book cover, English, 1613 This piece is not only dated, but it also bears the initials of Elizabeth Illingworthe. On the front cover it shows Abraham about to sacrifice Isaac, and on the back there is a scene of Jonah and the Whale. The embroidery is in silk on linen canvas, and it is worked in tent stitch, with some bullion stitch and a few french knots *Victoria and Albert Museum, London*

ledge, built out from the wall of a room, or set into the recess of a window, or was in the form of long wooden benches. Cushions, many of which measured 42 in. in length x 22 in. in width (106 cm x 56 cm), were, therefore, made to place on these long seats, with some square cushions for fitting into corners. There were also cushion kneelers for the bed-chamber, and cushions for placing in the stalls of cathedrals and churches, and in college chapels and libraries. Tiny tent stitch cushions were made to support the Bible and other special books, or for titled people to use as a base on which to place a crown or coronet. There were also christening cushions on which the baby was rested during the ceremony, and cushions for dining stools.

Often very small tent stitch cushions were specially adorned with tassels of silk and metal thread, and these were considered ideal gifts for giving to special friends at the New Year. One such cushion had been worked in the previous century by Princess Elizabeth as a gift for her governess, and in 1598 a German visitor to England, named Paul Hentzner, mentions having seen it at Windsor, a cushion 'most curiously wrought by Elizabeth's own hand.'[1] During the seventeenth century similar very small cushions, worked on fine canvas, were still being embroidered in silk, or silk and metal thread.

The larger, oblong cushions were worked mainly in tent stitch, but sometimes they also included cross stitch and long-legged cross stitch as well, and they were worked in wool with only the high-lights in silk. The one illustrated shows a coat-of-arms surrounded by flowers and leaves. It is worked entirely in tent stitch and carries the date 1604. Only the tops of such cushions were embroidered, the underside being covered with a cheaper material, which was sometimes velvet and sometimes simply a plain woven material. The stuffing used was feathers. This

---

[1] Hughes, Therle *English Domestic Needlework*, London, 1961.

Long cushion cover of the early seventeenth century In the centre of the design are the arms of James I and the initials I R, and the piece is signed Mary Hulton. Coloured silks and wools and silver-gilt thread have been used for the working in tent, plaited and long-legged cross stitches on linen canvas *Victoria and Albert Museum, London*

Long cushion cover, 1604 This cushion cover is 3 ft 6 in. in length and 22 in. (107 cm x 56 cm) wide and is worked in tent stitch with wool and silk on linen canvas. The design shows a shield with the arms of Hereford, enclosed by a wreath of small flowers, from which spread other circling stems with large flowers, among which are the letters I R (Jacobus Rex)
Victoria and Albert Museum, London

Sketch of a chair at Holyrood Palace, English, early seventeenth century. This piece consists of Turkey-work in coloured wools on a background of flat stitches in black silk

Sketch of an early seventeenth century English Turkey-work cushion

Sketch of an early seventeenth century design for a Turkey-work cushion

practice of using embroidery only for decorating the top surface of a cushion was general right down to the twentieth century, and it resulted from the fact that canvas work was always regarded as an expensive craft, which was used to produce luxury articles. This idea arose not only because of the high cost of the materials used in doing this work, but more importantly because it involved a labour of numerous hours in order to produce a good finished piece.

Fully upholstered chairs

The seventeenth century saw the development of the production of fully upholstered chairs. Before that time only a limited number of such chairs had been in use, and these had been generally reserved solely for the heads of families. In very early days rooms had contained hardly any furniture at all: only one chair would have been in each room, with wooden benches forming the normal seating for most persons, and a wooden plank placed on trestles was used as the table. The latter would have had a cover thrown over it, which would in some cases have been embroidered. Even in state apartments only one chair of state would have been placed in a room. This would have had a cover in embroidery placed over it and would have had a canopy, which would also have been richly embroidered, in position above it. The table in the early state apartments would have been just like those in other homes, a wooden plank, placed upon trestles, but it would probably have been covered with a richly embroidered table cover.

During the Stuart period in England the shape of chairs underwent a considerable change: the earlier chairs and benches were replaced in the course of time by a much more solid and comfortable type of chair, and the long cushions, which had been so necessary in the earlier days, gave way to fully upholstered chairs. The needle-work coverings, which were often done in Turkey work, were fixed permanently to the backs and the seats of the chairs with gilt studs.

Samplers

The name sampler is derived from the Latin exemplar, which meant a pattern or model, an example to work from, and the earliest samplers were presumably purely utilatarian, rather than decorative. Their place of origin in this country may have been the professional workshops, where they were used as teaching aids for the benefit of the apprentices, who were thus able to familiarise themselves with stitches and stitch patterns.

We know that samplers were worked here in the sixteenth century, and according to literary sources some were probably made even earlier. In the Privy Purse expenses of Queen Elizabeth of York, dated 1502, there is a reference to samplers in an item which reads: 'the Xth day of July, to Thomas Fische in reward for bringing of conserve of cherys from London to Windsore . . . and for an elne of lynnyn cloth for a sampler for the Queen, viij d (8 pence)'. The poet Skelton, who lived from 1469 to 1529, mentions in a poem, written in about 1504, 'the saumpler to sow on, the lacis to enbraid'. Shakespeare makes reference to samplers in two of his plays. In *Titus Andronicus*, which is thought to have been written in 1593, Marcus Andronicus, on finding in Act II Scene 4 that his niece Lavinia has been savagely mutilated, states that her case is even worse than that of Philomela, who had had her tongue cut out, but who was still able to record what had been done to her by working a message in embroidery on a sampler:

Fair Philomel, why she but lost her tongue,
And in a tedious sampler sew'd her mind:
But lovely niece, that mean is cut from thee;
A craftier Tereus, cousin, hast thou met,
And he hath cut those pretty fingers off,
That could have better sew'd than Philomel.

Shakespeare also refers to the working of samplers in *A Midsummer Night's Dream*, which is held to have been written in the period from 1594 to 1595. In Act III Scene 2 Helena says to Hermia:

O, is all forgot?
All school-days' friendship, childhood
    innocence?
We, Hermia, like two artificial gods,
Have with our needles created both one flower,
Both on one sampler, sitting on one cushion,
Both warbling of one song, both in one key;
As if our hands, our sides, voices, and minds,
Had been incorporate.

The working of samplers must have been very popular from quite early in the seventeenth century, as in 1613, the tenth year of the reign of James I, a certain Thomas Milles complained bitterly about the working of samplers and pleaded with women to 'Fear God and learn woman's housewifery, not idle samplery or silken follies'. Could it have been that he was having difficulty with his women folk in the running of the household?

A few very early samplers are thought to have

Detail of a sampler of the early seventeenth century, worked in silk on fine linen canvas. This sampler shows the early use of rococo stitch for the working of flowers and fruit and several attractive repeat patterns for the working of small objects such as bags, purses and small cushions, as well as boxes

The Mamluk Sampler Egyptian of uncertain date, but thought to be between 1250 and 1517 AD. Three fragments are roughly sewn together. Darning and double-running stitches are used in dark blue and natural linen thread on linen with a mesh of 28 threads to one inch (25 mm) *Guildford Corporation*

been worked in mediaeval times. These have been recovered from Egyptian burial grounds of that period and are all worked in double-running stitch. They are samplers of pattern darning and also of decorative patterns, based on the lozenge and on the S and X motifs, which are so familiar to us on the early seventeenth century English samplers. This clearly suggests that the embroiderers of the West were still being greatly influenced at this time by Near Eastern work, the design elements of which reached them via Italy. These Egyptian samplers had been made for the very same purpose as those which were worked in the West: they were examples of patterns to be used both for mending and for marking, not only articles of personal wear, but also household linen.

The Bostocke Sampler, English, 1598   This is the earliest known dated sampler   *Victoria and Albert Museum, London*

Portion of a sampler, worked in coloured silks on linen by Frances Bridon, aged 10. English, dated 31st October, 1644 *Fitzwilliam Museum, Cambridge*

The earliest dated English sampler that we possess bears the date 1598. It was found in 1960 and is now safely preserved in the Victoria and Albert Museum. This sampler, which is signed JANE BOSTOCKE, was obviously worked to commemorate the birth of a child, as the inscription states in capital letters, which are worked in back stitch, ALICE: LEE: WAS: BORNE: THE: 23: OF: NOVEMBER: BEING: TWESDAY: IN: THE: AFTER: NOON: 1596. Of the many other samplers still in existence in Britain the majority are unfortunately undated, and this makes it exceedingly difficult to place them in any sort of chronological order. Two obviously early samplers, however, which are thought to have been worked in the first part of the sixteenth century, are a German example and an Italian one. These were probably worked at about the same time as the printed pattern books came into being, and when the working of ecclesiastical embroidery started to decline.

These new pattern books were exceedingly rare and were only available to the very wealthy members of society, so that, when they had been worked on canvas, the different patterns were quickly copied by every woman who was lucky enough to come into contact with them. In this way the designs were spread in the course of time over the whole of the continent of Europe, and this fact accounts for the great similarity which is noticeable in the samplers worked in various European countries.

Quite early in the seventeenth century there appears to have been a complete change in the method of working samplers: in place of the fairly wide rectangular ones with their numerous small, detached stitch patterns, worked at random over an area of fine linen canvas in polychrome silk and gold and silver thread, there now appeared much longer and narrower samplers, some of which measured as much as one yard in length, but no more than seven or eight inches in width. They were worked with many horizontal bands of repeat-patterns in varying widths of from one to three inches upon a fine hand-woven canvas. The designs used no longer show the naturalistic renderings of flowers, which were a feature of the Elizabethan period, but have become much more formal in a style which is typical of the reign of James I and shows a definite Italian influence. Particular features which appear in these long samplers are that the bands of pattern worked across them are clearly taken from border-patterns, and the designs contain numerous funny little figures, which have come to be known in modern times as Boxers. No one appears to know exactly what these figures, which were common on samplers throughout the seventeenth and eighteenth centuries, represent, but Leigh Ashton, writing in his book on Samplers, says, 'they have their immediate prototypes in Italian and Spanish work of the late sixteenth and early seventeenth centuries, where the close connection with the putti of the Renaissance can be more plainly seen.'[1] These little figures always appear in exactly the same position, walking sideways with their faces either looking straight in front of them or perhaps glancing over their shoulders. They are male children, shown either naked or occasionally

---

[1] Ashton, Leigh *Samplers*, Medici Society, 1926.

Sketch of Boxer figures These are on oft-recurring motif on English seventeenth and eighteenth century samplers. The word 'boxer', which is an obvious misnomer, is a modern expression used by collectors to describe these figures. They are generally depicted nude, or very lightly clad, and the small scrolls, which emerge from the bodies of the little figures, are thought to be the last vestiges of a sword

clothed in the dress of the period, and they are depicted bearing some form of trophy or gift.

In the early sixteenth century Italian and other European examples of embroidery, showing scenes in which such little figures as the so-called Boxers appear, male and female figures alternate, and often they seem to depict scenes in which lovers are exchanging gifts. In the seventeenth century English samplers, however, all the female figures appear to have undergone a complete transformation: they are no longer recognisable as women, but appear instead as trees or flowering bushes. Traces of a head and various limbs can occasionally be seen and sometimes a head appears sprouting sprays of acorns.

The nature of samplers and the way in which they have been worked has differed greatly over the long period of time — some four hundred years — during which they have been regularly produced. At first, if we judge solely by the one early English example, dated 1598, patterns worked in silk and metallic threads in a variety of stitches were placed at random over the surface of the canvas. Plaited stitch, Interlacing stitch,

Buttonhole stitch, French knots, Bullion stitch, Tent stitch, Cross stitch and Satin stitch were the principal stitches used. Many more stitches, such as *point d'Hongrie*, Florentine, Romanian, Guilloche, Chain, Long-legged Cross and Algerian, were added to the list as the years rolled by, so that the embroiderers had by the end of the seventeenth century built up a considerable collection of stitches which they could call upon.

A fine, even-weave linen canvas was the material upon which the early samplers were worked. This material was often woven to the size required on a small loom, kept in the house of the person doing the sampler. In this way it became possible to produce quite easily the pieces of background canvas with the unusual length and narrow width which is a typical feature of many of the seventeenth century samplers. The workers were able to calculate the length and breadth of the canvas needed to suit their requirements by first deciding the number of border-patterns they wished to embroider and working out how many inches would be used for patterns in coloured silk and how much for the lace or white work examples they wished to include. A section of cut work and drawn thread work, combined with one containing white work, embroidered in Satin stitch in diaper patterns, was a definite part of most of the samplers produced in the first half of the seventeenth century, when lace and ruffs were popular wear. It is rare to find a dated sampler of this type as late as 1700, when the wearing of ruffs had ceased to be fashionable.

At some time towards the middle of the seventeenth century it seems to have become the custom to include upon samplers a representation of the alphabet and the numerals from one to ten. This happened at first only occasionally, and the alphabets were but roughly constructed. Full names were likewise rarely worked on early samplers, the embroiderers being content simply to give their initials, all of which suggests that these were the work of adults. Soon, however, we know that children were busily employed working samplers in school or under the instruction of their governesses. This is the time when we find alphabets and numerals becoming a routine requirement, and also, in addition to the date of the work, the full names and ages of the children were included. Sometimes the name of the teacher was also added, this being quite usual on Spanish samplers, as well as on a few of the English ones. It seems that samplers were generally worked at school by girls between the ages of five and fifteen years. The training of children to work the alphabet and numbers upon their samplers may have been the teachers' way of demonstrating that the children had learnt these facts, but it is thought that the real reason was to provide girls with a record of the method of working the letters of the alphabet and figures, so that, when they grew up and married, they would have something to guide them in marking the numerous pieces of linen that the well-to-do people were able to acquire in those days. For whatever reason, however, these samplers were treasured possessions to be carefully looked after, and when the owners died, they were often bequeathed by will to relations or friends.

Samplers continued to be made in England during the Cromwellian era: one, which bears the text, 'The feare of God is an excellent gift,' was worked by Martha Salter in 1651 and is at present in the Victoria and Albert Museum.

As is the case with the small contemporary pictures, seventeenth century samplers, which commemorate specific public events, are very rare. There is one, however, which is now in the Maidstone Museum, which does so: it was worked by Martha Wright in 1693, and it carries the following inscription: 'the Prince of Orange landed in the West of England on the 5th of November 1688 and on the 11th April 1689 was crowned King of England, and in the year 1692 the French came to invade England and a fleet of ships sent by King William drove them from the English seas and took, sunk and burned twenty one of their ships.'

Obviously this was a series of events, which had impressed the young mind of Martha Wright.

One year later, in 1694, Mary Minshall embroidered on her sampler the following inscription:

There was an earthquake,
On the 8 of September 1692
in the City of London
But no hurt tho it
caused most part
of England to tremble.

American canvas work

When the Mayflower sailed from England in the year 1620, the Puritans took with them to the New World the knowledge of the arts and crafts of their old country, which, of course, included weaving and embroidery. The seeds thus planted in the virgin soil grew in the course of time and flourished. As would be expected, however, the work of the New England ladies was very much in the old English style they knew so well, and it continued thus for some time, although the designs became less sophisticated, and the method of working the stitches was modified in order to save thread. In the meantime new ideas for embroidery designs in Europe came and went in rapid succession, whilst the New England embroideresses continued working in the styles they had brought with them long after the fashion for them had disappeared in Europe.

Many American probate records contain references to Turkey work. One such reference alludes to the furniture in the hall of Governor John Haynes of Hartford, Connecticut, who died in the year 1653, as 'velvet chairs, Turkey wrought chairs and a green cloth carpet for the table'. There are many other such references between 1640 and 1700, so that it is clear that a fashion in furnishings, which had been popular in England long before the Puritans left for America, remained in favour with them for many years afterwards.

The fashion for raised-work caskets and mirror frames and for the very fine tent stitch pictures and tiny cushions, which had been so popular in Britain at the start of the seventeenth century, had come to an end here about 1680. In America, however, such things first became popular at a much later date — possibly around 1700 — and enjoyed during the following century a heyday, which lasted apparently from about 1750 to as late as 1790.

The first person thought to have made a canvas

work sampler in America was Loara Standish. She was born in the year 1623 of English parents, her father being Myles Standish, one of the Pilgrim Fathers, who had been a soldier in the Netherlands, and who became military defender of New Plymouth. Loara's sampler, which she made at the age of about ten years, contains the following verse:

> Loara Standish is my Name.
> Lord Guide my Hart that I may do Thy Will,
> Also Fill my hands with such convenient Skill
> As may conduce to Virtue Void of Shame,
> And I will give the Glory to Thy Name.

After the great hardships experienced by the pioneers in America in the early years of the seventeenth century, the population had begun to grow, and by the end of that century and the beginning of the next the people were starting to acquire wealth. A substantial middle-class had emerged, which began the building of fine houses in which to display the treasures they had brought over from Europe. Sewing was considered a necessary achievement for all girls, just as it was in England, and the working of samplers was one of the first things a girl was taught. The first sampler she was instructed to make was a purely utilitarian article, consisting of the usual alphabet and numerals, but the second, more advanced piece was also a more sophisticated and decorative affair, a thing which was worthy of being framed and displayed on the walls of a wealthy American home. These samplers were lively and showed an independence of style, which made them far less formal than were their English counterparts.

Boxes and caskets

A firm favourite for covering with canvas embroidery during Stuart times was a jewel box: being flat and oblong, it had a simple shape, which was convenient for covering with panels of very fine canvas. Popular pictorial scenes were worked in tent stitch on the canvas panels mainly with silk thread, or sometimes the whole casket would be covered with beadwork, which was also very popular at the time. When all the pieces of canvas work were complete, they were sent to a cabinet maker for mounting.

In addition to simple jewel boxes of this type, more elaborate caskets were also very popular. Many of these were embroidered with raised work (what in Victorian times came to be known as stump work) on a background of ivory satin.

Lid of a Stuart casket, mid seventeenth century Rebekah is here seen giving a drink to the steward Eliezer. The covering is worked with silk mainly in tent stitch on linen canvas *Victoria and Albert Museum, London*

Stuart casket, mid seventeenth century The illustration shows the front doors of the casket. On the left-hand door the steward Eliezer is seen taking leave of Abraham in his tent. On the right-hand door he is on his journey to find Rebekah and is leading his camel
Victoria and Albert Museum, London

Nobody really knows why the fashion for this kind of work suddenly inspired so many embroiderers in England to sit down and spend hours of solid work in producing this most unusual of all the styles of embroidery that have come down to us. It may have reached here from Italy or Germany, as it appeared in both these countries at a very early date, but in both Italy and Germany the resultant work had a far more restrained appearance than the extravagant style the English embroiderers managed to produce. Nobody can call it beautiful, and some people consider it an abomination, while others, who are most probably embroiderers themselves, regard it as interesting and even fascinating, and marvel at the enormous amount of work and ingenuity involved, thinking, above all, what fun and enjoyment it must have given the workers to clothe the little padded figures in such elaborate clothes and to use all the many new stitches and materials in an endeavour to make them really lifelike.

While most of this raised work was embroidered on a background of ivory satin, there are some instances of its being worked on canvas, and many of the caskets, which were not worked entirely on canvas, had certain sections, which were worked on canvas and then applied to the satin back-

A drawing from a mid-seventeenth century canvas-work picture, showing a favourite subject for such work in those days, Elijah and the Widow of Zarephath (I Kings 17). The original of this drawing was worked in silk on a very fine canvas

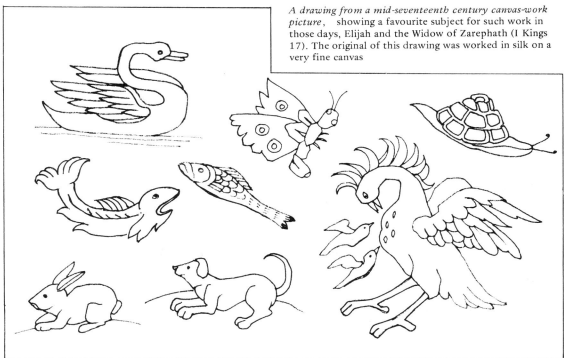

70

Collection of objects worked by Martha Edlin in the seventeenth century   The casket is worked in tent stitch and some other stitches on fine linen canvas, which has then been applied to a satin background material   *Victoria and Albert Museum, London*

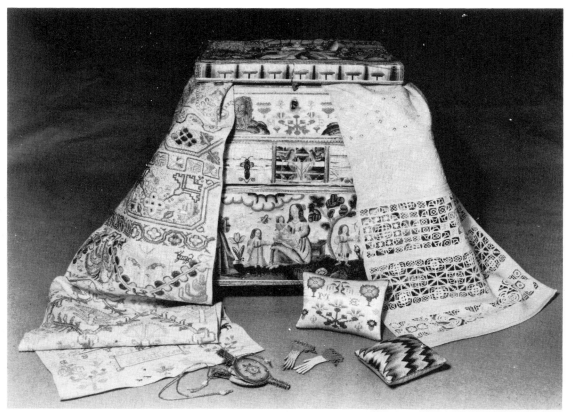

ground. It is interesting to note that those caskets, which were worked on canvas, seem to have avoided, in the same way as the small, canvas work pictures did, the extreme extravagances of much of the work done on ivory satin.

All these caskets were very similar in construction. They often contained little drawers and compartments, nicely lined with silk or coloured paper. The inside of the lid generally housed a treasured looking glass, and the box tray would have a place for ink bottles, a glass scent bottle and pounce boxes, as well as a container for sand and other items. The drawers, of course, generally included the small 'secret' drawer to hold the precious rings and jewels, or maybe a very special love-letter, and this was usually placed in position behind one of the other drawers, so that it must have been secret in name only. Tiny silver handles were attached to the drawers and also to the doors which sometimes enclosed them. These caskets were finally finished off with four ball-feet, which were made either of silver or of wood. An outer oak box was often provided, into which the casket could be placed, in order or protect it.

After the middle of the seventeenth century many children were taught embroidery, as we have seen, by the working of samplers. As a final stage in this embroidery tuition they were expected to show their proficiency in this art by working one of these caskets, a box or maybe a mirror surround in a style of embroidery, which they were allowed to choose for themselves.

A work box, English, 1692, thought to have been worked by Parnell Mackett, whose initials appear on the lid, The embroidery is done with silk in rococo and double-running stitches on linen canvas
Victoria and Albert Museum, London

Detail of lid of work box

Mirror surrounds

During the seventeenth century mirrors became an important item in the homes of the well-to-do. In early times most of the mirrors in existence seem to have been very small and in the form of pieces of polished steel, which were not only very scarce, but also very costly. When they were framed, it was usually in silver or ivory. There is a reference in the accounts of King Edward I in the fourteenth century to 'a comb and mirror of silver gilt,' and later in the privy purse expenses of Henry VIII, dated 1530, there is an entry concerning the payment to a Frenchman for 'Certayne looking-glasses'. This latter reference, although it sounds as if it might concern glass mirrors, is thought still to be describing polished steel mirrors, as it is rather unlikely that glass was actually used for this purpose before the end of the sixteenth century.

In this connection it is interesting to note that one of the new industrial activities of the reign of Elizabeth I was the manufacture of glass, but that this material was not available in the form of windows in middle-class homes until the reign of Charles I.

Although mirrors were now more common and were slightly larger than previously, they still remained small in comparison with those of succeeding generations and were enormously expensive. It became the custom, therefore, to surround them with wide, impressive frames,

Stuart mirror-surround, worked with silk, chenille and gimp on satin, and with some sections, which are worked on canvas in tent, rococo and buttonhole stitches, applied upon the satin background
Victoria and Albert Museum, London

covered with embroidery. The mirror itself was often enclosed first by the fitting of a narrow walnut or tortoise-shell frame. Then outside of this frame came the needlework panels, around which was placed an outer, narrow, wooden frame, which was carved, lacquered or sometimes simply edged with a braid of coloured silk or metallic thread. A few of these mirrors were also constructed so that they could be enclosed within two embroidered doors, in order that the glass could be protected.

The embroidered mirror surrounds of the Stuart period consisted mainly of areas of raised work on ivory satin, but a certain number of them were also worked in tent stitch with silk thread upon a fine linen canvas. The technique used in these pieces of canvas work reflected that of the small tent stitch pictures of the period: being worked in tent stitch, the designs look more restrained and far less exaggerated and flambouyant than do those embroidered in raised work. Very often the top section of the design depicts a manor house or a castle against a blue and fawn sky, with large birds flying around; the side panels often show figures of royalty, standing upon little hillocks; and the bottom border has at its centre, more often than not, an elaborate fountain with outsize fish swimming around its base or with a mermaid emerging from the water. The spaces at the corners of the mirror surrounds are filled with representations of the lion and the unicorn or of a leopard or a camel. This subject matter was sometimes varied with, for instance, religious figures replacing those of royalty in the side panels.

The more popular raised work mirror surrounds were worked on the same type of ivory satin that was used in the production of raised work caskets and pictures of this period. An interesting point about them is that the shapes of the surrounds, which were used for raised work embroidery, were generally much more complicated than were those used for covering with canvas work. This was presumably because the very pliable satin material used in raised work could be more easily mounted on such intricate shapes than could tent stitch embroidery on canvas.

The mid-seventeenth century

In spite of the continual political strife which occurred in England during the seventeenth century, and which included not only The Civil War, but also the execution of the monarch and the abolition of Parliament, the craft of embroidery experienced no interruption. The English Civil War was really a mild affair when compared with

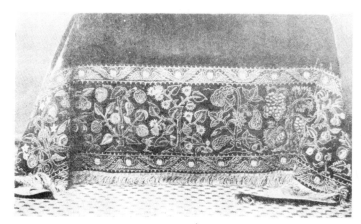

Altar cloth of the seventeenth century at Hollingbourne Church in Kent   Motifs worked on canvas have been applied to purple velvet. The Ladies Culpepper are thought to have worked this altar cloth during the Commonwealth period and presented it to the Church at the time of the Restoration
Hollingbourne Church, Maidstone, Kent

Altar cloth at Hollingbourne Church   A detail of one corner of this piece

the Thirty Years' War, which was raging on the continent of Europe at about the same time, and it was only to a very limited extent a class war. Unlike the French Revolution in the next century, which saw the uprising of a poor, oppressed people against the aristocratic ruling classes, the Civil War in England simply gave more power to the newly emerging middle classes, among whom were many people to whose efforts we owe the great increase in the production of embroidery at that time.

*Sketches of drawings published by John Overton
British Museum Print Room*

Contrary to what some might imagine would have been the state of affairs in England during the Puritan regime, and when Oliver Cromwell was the Lord Protector, embroidery and the arts and crafts in general were not adversely affected. Cromwell's mother was herself an ardent embroiderer, and this fact may have influenced his attitude. She is reported to have maintained at her own expense six clergymen's daughters, whom she employed on needlework projects in her own apartments.

It is interesting to note that the Commonwealth government also made many attempts to revive the manufacture of tapestries at Mortlake, which had been started in the reign of James I and had been handsomely supported by Charles I, only to fall upon bad times during the period of the troubles between the king and Parliament.

During this period in English history the amateur embroiderer was greatly helped in the preparation of suitable designs for her work by the publication of numerous books of engravings. One well-known publisher of such books was Peter Stent, who operated between 1643 and 1667 from his publishing house, which was situated at the sign of the White Horse in Giltspur Street in London. He was followed by John Overton, who continued with the same type of publication from the White Horse in Little Britain and also from the White Horse without Newgate, until he retired in 1707. Among the many books of engravings, which were published during this period, were *A New Book of Flowers, Beasts and Birds*, invented and drawn by J Dunstall; *A Book of Branches, Slips, Flies, etc*; *The Four Seasons of the Year*, made by W Hollar; *The Five Senses*, devised by Marmion; and *The Four Quarters of the World — Engravings of the Elements*. There were also printed pictures of Queen Elizabeth, King James and Queen Anne, and various other kings and queens, as well as well-known princes and dukes. These are but a few of the subjects listed in the trade sheets issued by Peter Stent, which contained in all some 500 titles, many of which could also be obtained in colour.

These illustrations were converted into embroidery both on canvas and on the ivory-coloured satin, that was so popular for the working of the fashionable raised work caskets of those days. Although it seems that all or most of the designs used for embroidery at this time, which show scenes from the Old Testament and from classical literature, must have been taken from engravings, it is difficult to pin-point the

Tent stitch panel, English, seventeenth century This was probably a table carpet, and it appears to have been worked on squares of canvas, which have been joined together to form the centre panel, which is surrounded by a border *Victoria and Albert Museum, London*

precise engraving that was used for a specific piece of work. The engravers themselves blatantly borrowed from all and sundry publications, and it was considered quite legitimate for the embroiderer, or any other craftsman, either to copy the engravings exactly, or to alter them by changing the position of the figures in the scenes they depicted, or by adding other figures or animals or flowers from other publications. Few of these engravings would, in fact, have been used by an embroiderer in the exact form in which they were originally published: they would have been mostly interpreted and adapted for the purpose by some intermediary, who would have produced a new drawing from which the final embroidery would have been worked.

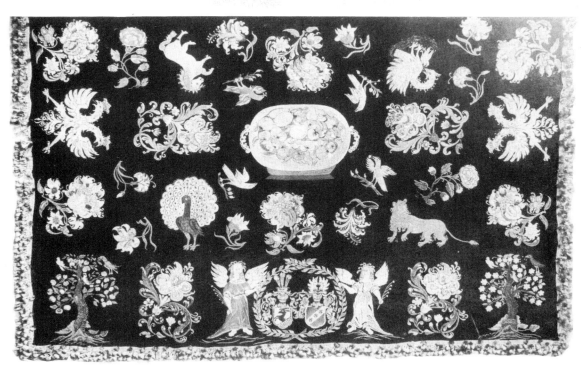

Table carpet, North German seventeenth century   This is probably a marriage table carpet, worked for Leopold I, the Holy Roman Emperor. The design shows two coats of arms within a wreath of laurel, a lion, which is looking very apprehensive, a very proud peacock, a central tureen, containing fruit (a sign of plenty) and two double-headed eagles, which latter would lead one to assume that there was a connection with the Hapsburgs. The carpet is beautifully finished with a bobble fringe

Picture, English, 1675-80   Worked with silk in tent, rococo and long and short stitches
Victoria and Albert Museum, London

The Restoration

The period of the Restoration of Charles II saw at first little change in the nature of the canvas embroidery that was then being worked. Later events, however, led on to a change of style. In 1665 London underwent the terrible ordeal of the Great Plague, which was undoubtedly brought about as a result of the unhygienic habits of those days, one of which was the sweeping of used rushes from the floors into the streets. As a result of the ravages of the plague such things as cushions and table carpets, which, it was thought, might have helped to spread the disease, were thrown out and burnt. The very next year the deadly Great Fire consumed the major part of the city and completed the destruction there of an enormous amount of embroidered furnishings. These events led to fresh thinking not only on hygiene, but also on the style of furnishings, so that the latter were not replaced by replicas of past work, but by pieces which showed a gradual development to new ideas in design.

One result of this new development in embroidery design during the later years of the Restoration period is seen in the production of large numbers of long 'Jacobean' curtains, which were used as hangings for the four-poster beds of the time. These curtains have designs, based on the large, flowing shapes of heavy plant stems and exotic leaves, which meander over the entire surface. They were worked entirely in wool on twill linen in crewel work, using numerous different stitches, and, although crewel work is outside the subject of this book, it must be mentioned here, because of the very definite influence it had at this time upon canvas work, causing a complete change in the designs which were used: in place of the small, detailed tent stitch pictures of the past, bold floral patterns, showing much larger flowers, were worked upon canvas and many new stitches were also introduced into the working.

The seventeenth century in France

During the seventeenth century in France Louis XIV, who was intensely interested in all forms of art, did much to encourage the production of embroidery. He not only gave employment to several skilled embroiderers in his household, but he also employed others at the Gobelin factory, where they were accommodated in premises

Summer, a French tent-stitch hanging of 1683-84 This ▷ is a large hanging, worked on canvas with wool and silk, and with a background of metal thread
The Metropolitan Museum of Art, New York

Sketch of tent-stitch picture, English, late seventeenth century Worked with silk and wool on fine canvas, this picture illustrates the story of the 'Disobedient Prophet' from the first Book of Kings, chapter 13. Size: 16 in. x 12½ in. (40 cm x 32 cm)

Floral panel in tent stitch, French, late seventeenth century This panel is thought to have been worked in the school founded in about 1680 in the village of St Cyr by Madame de Maintenon

adjoining the famous tapestry weavers' manufactory. We have the names of two of these embroiderers, Simon Fayette and Philibert Balland, who were responsible for the working of large wall-hangings and furnishings of all kinds, such as settee seats and backs, cushions and screens. The more difficult parts of the designs, such as the figures and animals, were apparently worked by Fayette, whilst Balland was responsible for working the plants and the rest of the background, which was considered to be rather less skilled work. This procedure of the more highly skilled craftsmen working the figures, with the less skilled workers and the apprentices doing the donkey work, has been general practice all down the ages in professional workshops.

Madame de Maintenon, a former mistress of

Louis XIV, who at the age of fifty eventually married the French King, had founded in about 1680 a school in the village of St Cyr, some thirteen miles from Paris, where young ladies of good birth, whose parents had fallen upon evil times, could be taught the art of embroidery. The training course lasted for three years, and later, when the girls became sufficiently skilled, they worked many pieces of canvas work, together with other types of embroidery, to be used as hangings and for covering furniture such as sofas, chair seats and backs, cushions, screens and many other things. These various furnishings were made to order for the purpose of replenishing the stock of furniture and other adornments in the royal palaces and adding further new items to it. Her last years were passed at St Cyr, where she died in 1719 at the age of 84.

In about the year 1683 an attempt was made in France to persuade the Chinese to embroider on canvas copies of the tremendously expensive Gobelin tapestries. It would appear that it was considered more economical to get this work done in the Far East rather than in France.

Trade was developing greatly at this time between countries of the West and those in the Far East. The contact with the Far East had been started long before this time, in the first place by the Portuguese and Dutch merchants during the late fifteenth century, and then by the setting up of the English and Dutch East India Companies in the early seventeenth century, so that, although the French Compagnie de la Chine was not founded until 1660, people in France had already developed a strong liking for Chinoiserie as a result of the fact that foreign ships had been bringing into their country over many years previously a variety of articles from China and India.

The arrival of the Chinese style in Europe caused the production of some work of an unusual extravagance by native designers, with the exception of the French, who, being rather more conservative in nature, avoided the extravagances of their neighbours and produced designs that were more decoratively restrained and showed an improvement, for instance, over contemporary English work, particularly in the drawing of the figures. The French received this new style of Eastern design with open arms and finally moulded it to their own liking in a way that led on to the development in the early eighteenth century of that delicate Rococo style, which, while being definitely French, still retained its original Chinese character. It was both decorative and elegant, but,

nevertheless, it remained popular only for a short time.

Torah curtain, Italian, dated 1676-1703 This curtain is worked in straight stitches on fine canvas
Victoria and Albert Museum, London

William and Mary

A great change in all aspects of embroidery in England was brought about when the Roman Catholic, James II, was forced to leave the country in 1688, and the Protestants, William of Orange and his wife Mary, were invited to become joint monarchs of Britain. They brought with them the oriental style of embroidery design, which had been popular in Holland for some time previously, and which was soon accepted with equal favour on this side of the Channel. Canvas work designs,

83

Sketch of a detail from a tent-stitch panel, English, late seventeenth century

reflecting paintings of flowers by Dutch artists, were also introduced. These floral designs show a noticeable difference from earlier work in that the flowers and leaves depicted are much bigger and bolder. They are also beautifully shaded, being worked in wool in tent stitch, with silk used to render the highlights. Works of this kind were in general well-designed and executed, the canvas used being of a somewhat coarser mesh than that formerly used, in order to accommodate the bolder designs.

Sketch of another detail from the tent-stitch panel of the late seventeenth century   This detail depicts the figure of Justice opposed to Vanity and Malice

In addition to these largely floral designs, canvas work of the late seventeenth century also included examples of that strange mixture of oriental and Western styles, which has been called Chino-Dutch. This was a design, built up by using many interlocking abstract shapes, which was worked in a variety of colours mainly in gros point (tent stitch worked over two threads of the canvas) or cross stitch. These curious shapes would be used to surround a central panel of landscape with figures, which was worked in tent stitch.

Yet another type of design, which is related to this in style, is one where Chinese figures are scattered at random over the background: Chinese open parasols appear, which are often held firmly in the hands of a black boy, and large oriental flowers and abstract shapes entirely cover the ground. The figures alone are worked in tent stitch,

Drawing from a French Needlework panel   This panel shows the strong Chinese influence on French canvas work, which became popular in the late seventeenth century

and the rest of the canvas is worked in cross stitch. This kind of design was popular for covering some of the wing chairs of that period.

There was a considerable demand at this time for the covering of fully upholstered chairs, stools, settees, sofas and wing chairs, and canvas work became very popular for this purpose, as well as for covering screens, for it was not only a very decorative art, but also a very durable medium for the upholstering of furniture. Wool was now the principal fibre used in working on canvas, with only a small amount of silk being employed to lighten the effect. The canvas used was made of linen of a reasonably fine mesh with approximately 16 or 18 threads to the inch, and, when the embroidery was done in tent stitch, this reinforced the canvas and made it into one of the most durable of fabrics. It wore well and appeared to wear clean as well, only needing an occasional banging to dislodge any dust which may have accumulated. Canvas work has the advantage of not requiring the same care and attention, that has to be given to damask upholstery, which often involves complete replacement.

Sketch of a wing chair,   English of the late seventeenth Century, showing Samuel anointing David. The work is in tent stitch on linen canvas. From a chair in the *Judge Irwin Untermeyer Collection* in the *Metropolitan Museum of Art, New York*

Wing chair, English, late seventeenth century   Chinoiserie or Chino-Dutch design, worked here in gros-point (tent stitch worked over two threads of the canvas)

85

The popular needlework wing chairs were one of the outstanding achievements of the sevent4enth century. They were very handsomely designed and generally were beautifully worked, most of them entirely in tent stitch. Although it is not known whether they were produced professionally or not, the exceedingly high standard of work they reveal would suggest that it was done by professionals. The designs were specially planned to fit each individual chair. The whole chair would be covered in needlework, with the exception of the outside back of the chair and the underside of the cushion. The worked part of the apron would extend only from the front of the chair to six inches under the cushion. This means that only the visible parts of the chair would be worked in embroidery, the parts not seen being finished with a covering of cheaper woven fabric.

A design, which was popular for working on these wing chairs, was one based on a religious or classical scene with figures. The back of the chair and the seat carried the main subject matter, and the inside wings and arms might sometimes have a minor figure or two included on them, but they were used in the main just for landscape, as were the outside arms, the wings and cushion borders, while the arm facings and the apron often carried a flowing floral design.

Very occasionally during the time of William and Mary one might have come across needlework slip-over covers for single upholstered chairs, such as the set of five, worked in tent stitch, which

William and Mary chair-seat A piece of English work, which was carried out in tent stitch, using wool and a little silk for the highlights

can be seen in the Irwin Untermeyer Collection, New York.

The Hatton Garden Panels

There is in the Victoria and Albert Museum in South Kensington a set of six large canvas work panels, each one measuring approximately 7 ft 6 in. x 3 ft 10 in. (2.2 m x 1.2 m), which were discovered in 1896, hidden behind layers of wall paper and plaster, in an old, moderately sized house in Hatton Garden in London. When found, they were in an appallingly dirty condition, and it was only after they had been carefully cleaned and found to be in a good state of preservation, that it was realized what a remarkable treasure had come to light, after lying hidden for over two hundred years.

The design of these panels is bold and shows pillars with Corinthian capitals, which support semi-circular arches, and up which sinewy stems, bearing giant flowers and massive leaves, entwine themselves, until they reach the top, where exotic Eastern birds disport themselves among the rich foliage. Animals recline at the base of each panel. The basic design of the pillars and the semi-circular archway is repeated on each panel, but each one varies in the detail of the animals, birds and flowers, which are shown. The animals depicted include the deer, squirrel, fox, sheep, elephant, camel, lion, horse, goat, dog, leopard, unicorn and a magnificent winged dragon.

The fact, that the designs used in these Hatton Garden Panels are related to those of the large crewel work curtains of the seventeenth century, is revealed in the exotic birds, the large flowers and the wide-veined, curly leaves, all of which appear to be based upon the painted cotton palampores, imported by the East India Company, which had been coming into this country from the early years of the century onwards.

The panels are worked in wool in a remarkable number of different stitches, including in addition to tent stitch such other stitches as cross stitch, satin stitch, brick stitch, Rococo stitch and french knots. Nobody knows for certain when they were worked, but it is thought to have taken place at some time in the last quarter of the seventeenth century. It does seem possible that they could have been commissioned from a firm dealing with embroidery, which is known to have been in existence at this time in the vicinity of St Paul's in London, an area in which the principal print-makers and the publishers of embroidery designs carried on their business.

Hatton Garden Panel   This is one of a set of six long
canvas-work panels, each measuring 7 ft 6 in. x 3 ft 10 in.
(2.2 m x 1.2 m). They are worked with wool in a wide
variety of stitches   *Victoria and Albert Museum, London*

The eighteenth century

Queen Anne

The influence of oriental art upon designs used for canvas work, which had become apparent in the decling years of the seventeenth century, continued into the early years of the eighteenth century and on throughout the reign of Queen Anne. At the same time, however, a new and very different style emerged, which was a complete contrast: instead of the large, flowing lines and gigantic flowers and leaves, such as are seen in the Hatton Garden panels, designs consisting of small flowers and leaves, portrayed in a way which shows a much greater leaning towards naturalism, began to find favour and continued unabated into the reign of George I and of George II.

A splendid example of this particular style is the Hatfield Carpet, which dates from the mid-eighteenth century, and is one of the most

Floral panel, English, early eighteenth century, embroidered in tent stitch with a cross stitch background, using wool and silk on a linen canvas

beautiful English needlework carpets ever worked. It is a small carpet by present-day standards and is worked entirely in tent stitch, with the addition of only a few french knots for the centres of the flowers. The design consists of a large panel of flowers, all radiating from a centrally placed sunflower, and this is surrounded by a border of other flowers. Honeysuckle, daffodils, irises, passion-flowers, carnations and many others are depicted on this carpet, and the result is a glorious array of outstanding natural beauty. This carpet and many others of the period bear the mark of the professional worker, but there are a few which are signed and may have been the work of amateurs, although even the signed and dated examples could have been commissioned to include this information. While most are worked with the traditional tent stitch, there are a few carpets of this time which also contain some cross stitch, chain stitch or long-legged cross stitch.

The first quarter of the new century saw an immense increase in the amount of canvas work

Folding card table with its top worked in tent stitch on canvas, using a floral design which is typical of the Queen Anne period. Such floral designs gave way later to designs which included playing cards

Spanish carpet of the seventeenth or eighteenth century The size is 9 ft 7 in. x 4 ft 6 in. (2.8 m x 1.3 m). This carpet is a fine example of canvas work carried out with wool on a coarse canvas ground
Victoria and Albert Museum, London

Design for the top of an eighteenth century card table to be worked in tent stitch. The drawing shows fish-counters and money, together with playing cards

Map of England sampler,   signed and dated Ann Gardiner, 17th March, 1792. This sampler is worked with silk on woollen canvas, and the stitches used are tent stitch, cross stitch and some eyelets. This was a popular type of sampler to work in the last quarter of the eighteenth century
Victoria and Albert Museum, London

produced for furnishings, which were worked mainly in tent stitch and sometimes also in cross stitch. Settees with sets of matching chairs, which had drop-in seats, were now exceedingly popular, and, if all the so-called Queen Anne chairs were really worked in the short period of twelve years of that queen's reign, then the embroiderers of those days must indeed have been a truly industrious body of people. In addition hinged folding card tables, with their tops worked in tent stitch on canvas, first came into use at this time. Gambling had always been a great pastime among the wealthy people in England and they certainly must have made use of playing-cards for very many years previous to this time. It, therefore,

Cheval fire-screen   of the period of William and Mary with a tent-stitch embroidered panel, worked in wool and silk. The blue and white bowl containing the flowers shows a distinct Chinese element, which was a feature of much of the decorative work of the time. In the possession of *Lady (John J.) Smith* at the *Bower House, Havering-atte-Bower, Essex*

90

Sketch of tent-stitch mirror-surround of the early eighteenth century

displayed designs either of flowers or of landscapes. The floral designs sometimes have bunches of flowers tastefully tied with ribbons, or they show a basket or vase containing flowers. A Chino-Dutch type of blue and white bowl containing flowers and standing upon a marble-topped table was another popular design for this purpose.

Although the reign of Queen Anne was short, it was important for at least one long-lasting innovation: it saw the birth of journalism in the work of Joseph Addison and Richard Steele, who produced between them in the period 1709 to 1712 the two famous journals known as the *Tatler* and the *Spectator*. These contained essays on a wide variety of subjects, which had the effect of opening up the flood-gates to a further enormous output of such writing, so that before long all the important publishers were issuing journals and magazines, which were to become the forerunners of the magazines of today.

In 1749 the *Ladies Magazine* came into being, having been founded by Jasper Goodwill of Oxford, who included designs for embroidery as supplements to the magazine. The designs were for all types of embroidery, but in an issue dated 1776 it is thought that a lesson in geography might

seems surprising to find that it was not until the reign of Queen Anne that folding card tables with tent stitch tops first came into use.

Many small articles, such as pincushions and bags of various kinds, continued to be worked on canvas. Small hand screens, which were needed to protect the face from the heat of the open fire or from unwelcome draughts of air, were also worked by keen embroiderers at this time. Not just one or two, but several of these small screens would be left lying around ready for use in the large reception rooms. Pole screens were also considered necessary for the same reason, and there are still numbers of them in existence, a fact which goes to prove how popular they were in their day. They were not only nice objects to work, being of a convenient size, but they could be extremely decorative, and at the same time very useful and necessary objects to have in a room. A moderately large, easily moveable screen of this type would be placed in a position for all to admire, and, as it was not subject to wear and tear in the way that embroidered chairs and stool tops were, it retained its beautiful appearance over many years, another fact that would account for its popularity. In the early years of the eighteenth century these screens

Sketch of a tent-stitch armchair, English work from the third quarter of the eighteenth century

Sketches of a tent-stitch picture of the eighteenth century, showing the squire and his family. *Sketch 1* is a detail of the left-hand side of the picture and shows a proud squire with four of his children. The inclusion of the family dog in the picture appears, however, to have presented an insurmountable problem to the designer.

be acceptable to the ladies, and the suggestion is made to the readers that, as 'one method that would probably answer that purpose, the map of England is recommended to the consideration of the ladies. It should be executed in needlework on canvas, which may afterwards be applied to the purpose of a fire-screen or framed for an ornament to a room'. The suggestion ends with the encouraging remark that 'the executive part will be far

from difficult'. It seems that this suggestion was acceptable to the ladies, as some three months later it was not a map of England, but 'an elegant map of Europe for needlework' which was issued.

The love of the English for floral patterns, which is so noticeable over the years, had blossomed once more with renewed vigour during the reign of Queen Anne and continued unabated into the reign of George I. Pastoral scenes, enclosed within a surround of flowers, were worked on chair seats, cushions, candle sconces and fire screens. Many sets of chairs were covered with needlework with an all-over floral design in which the flowers were shown radiating from one central flower. Other designs showed bunches of flowers tied with ribbons, and were similar in style to the

Sketch 2 is a detail of the right-hand side of the picture and shows the wife of the squire and the remaining three children

Sketch detail from an early eighteenth century tent-stitch picture, showing a waggoner with his cart and horses.

gold shade — which was used to highlight all the other colour ranges. The actual colours used were brighter in the eighteenth century than were those used in the previous century.

Needlework pictures contined to be popular throughout the eighteenth century, but there was a marked lowering in the standard of the design used. The life of the middle classes had by now been greatly improved, but, strange as it may seem, their pastimes seldom, if ever, appear as a subject for tent stitch pictures. The country squire, with his lady and his family around him, is, however, often portrayed as the focal point of a picture. He is seen carefully positioned in front of a well-drawn, red brick house, viewing with obvious pride the rural activities of his numerous work people, as they perform their duties all around him: the milkmaid milking a cow; the woodman carrying bundles of freshly-chopped wood; young people dancing around a maypole; the carrier returning home with his horse and cart. It is a real picture of activities of all kinds, for not only are many human beings shown taking part in what goes on, but dogs, sheep, rabbits and extra large birds are liberally scattered all over the surrounding landscape. Other very popular subjects at this time for designs in canvas work, which was still carried out mainly in tent stitch, were the pastoral scenes in which elegantly dressed figures, masquerading as

Sheperdess spinning wool A detail from an eighteenth century tent-stitch panel

French woven tapesty seat coverings of the period. Many others had baskets and vases containing conventional flowers. Now, in contrast to the very large flowers previously worked, all the flowers and leaves were small and, being worked in the usual tent stitch, were all very carefully shaded. There appear to have been very rigid rules governing the method of shading, which does not seem to have changed much all down the ages. Five shades of each colour were usually employed, plus one shade of either fawn silk, which was used to highlight the blue, blue-green, rose, mauve and fawn ranges, or yellow silk — either a lemon or a

Sketch from an eighteenth century chair, showing a gentleman dressed in contemporary costume, who is masquerading as a love-lorn shepherd and a sheperdess is seen here, complete with crown, fan and crook

94

shepherds and shepherdesses, are seen idly re-clining at ease with a dog by their sides and their peaceful flock of woolly sheep, all decked out in french knots, enjoying the sweet pastures. The fact that it was always the activities of the well-to-do upper classes, which were portrayed in such embroidered pictures, simply reflects the strong appeal which such events had for the engravers and publishers, who continued to supply designs for craftspeople of all kinds.

Although, as we have seen, tent stitch still remained the principal stitch used in canvas work at this time, Florentine stitch, or point d'hongrie, as it was then called, had a period of popularity in the middle years of the eighteenth century, when it became widely used on canvas, but it was now worked in crewel wool, which had replaced the silk thread formerly used for this stitch.

Sketch of a Detail from a Tent-stitch Picture of the early eighteenth century, showing peasants dancing around a maypole

Very few large canvas work panels were pro-duced after the reign of George I, but there was one notable canvas worker by the name of Mary Holt, who worked two large wall hangings and a carpet in cross stitch and tent stitch, which are now at Aston Hall in Birmingham. These she signed and dated 'Mary Holt, spinster, aged 60, 1744'.

Most of the other canvas work done at this time appears to have been in the form of small panels of tent stitch, which were applied on to a different background fabric, such as velvet or some other woven material. Sometimes a piece of canvas with a design already traced upon it would be tacked down on to this other fabric, and the working would then be taken through both the canvas and the background material. When the work was completed, the threads of the canvas would be withdrawn, so it was absolutely necessary to use loosely woven fine thread, canvas, in order to be able to adopt this particular method of working.

This use of canvas merely as the means for applying panels of embroidery upon another basic fabric was one element which led to the gradual decline in the production of good examples of canvas work during the second half of the eighteenth century. Another element also associated with this trend was provided by the architects of those days, some of whom were designers and makers of furniture, as well as being designers of buildings. A large number of houses were built at this time in a more modern style than any previously built, and the influence of the architects who designed them led to their also being furnished in a new, modern style.

There was an enormous number of very talented and creative craftsmen active in those days, and included among them were several eminent cabinet-makers and furniture designers, such as Thomas Chippendale, William Vile, the Adam Brothers, William Kent, George Hepplewhite, Thomas Sheraton and Thomas Shearer. Unlike the situation which exists today, there was very little specialisation in the eighteenth century, so that a man such as William Kent could not only be a well-known painter, but a good architect and designer of furniture as well.

Chippendale was considered by many experts to have been the foremost among the furniture designers. He published the first edition of his de luxe catalogue for the trade, called *The Gentleman and Cabinet-maker's Director*, in 1754. Two other editions followed, one in 1759, and another in 1762 with additional drawings. This book had a tremendous effect on the design of furniture: up to that time it had remained very traditional throughout the country, but with the publication of the *Director* new designs caught on everywhere. Chippendale's influence extended not only all over Britain, but also into Europe and as far afield as to America, the designs of his chairs in particular being considered his greatest achievement.

It was probably as a result of all this creativity among the furniture designers, however, that from this time onwards a rapid decline occurred in the

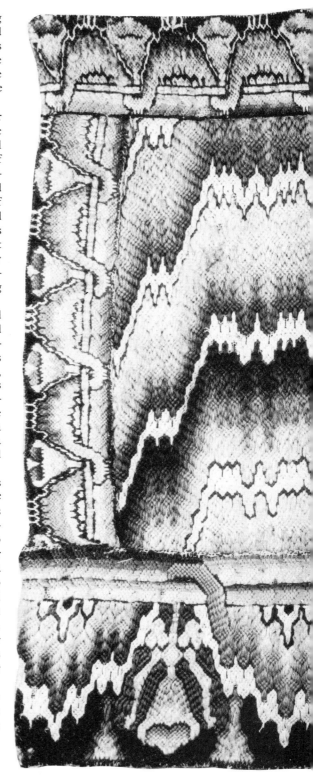

An eighteenth century example of point d'hongrie
Victoria and Albert Museum, London

96

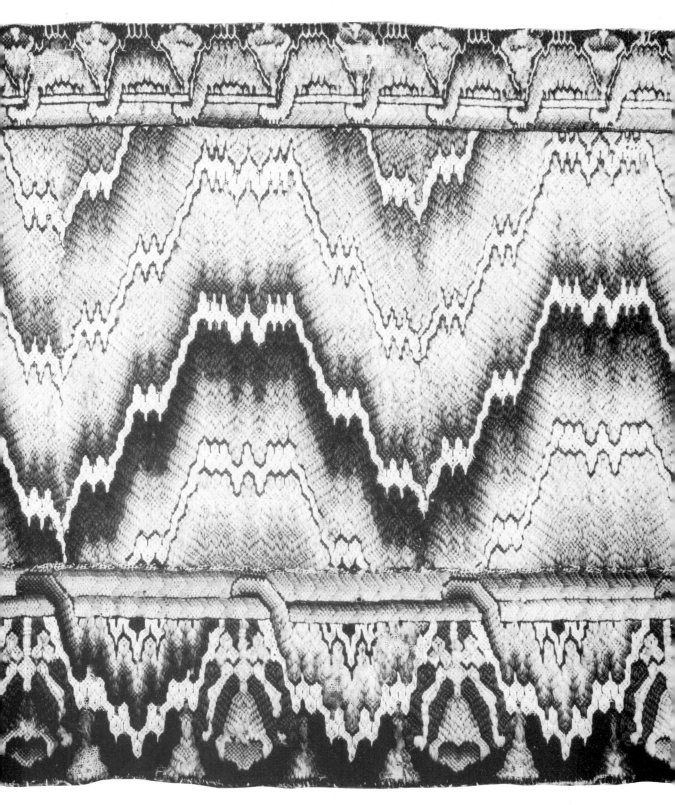

The Gardener and the Hog, one of a set of six chair seats worked in wool and silk in tent stitch and cross stitch. The centre designs for these chairs were taken from the illustrations, which were drawn by J Wootton and William Kent for Gay's *Fables*, first published in 1727

production of canvas work in England. The designs for the new chairs no longer envisaged the use of the old traditional coverings, and the young ladies of the day were in any case unprepared to spend hour after hour slavishly working such covers for settees and chairs.

The age of elegance had arrived, which meant that the whole of the interiors of the great houses had to be re-designed, and this entailed sweeping away all the old furniture, in order to make room for the delicate new style which was being established. The older chairs with their beautiful tent stitch coverings were now replaced with completely new ones, such as the Adam chairs, the seats of which were upholstered in the beautiful, but fragile figured silks, which were then being produced in France and Italy, and also here in Spitalfields, where there was a thriving silk manufactory. Other examples of the new style chairs were covered with marvellous silk brocades, woven tapestry or damasks. In addition to this, Hepplewhite decided that 'mahogany chairs should have the seats of horsehair, plain, striped, chequered, etc'.[1] Horsehair was being woven at the time in a wide range of patterns, including herringbone, and also in many different colours. It was, therefore, used extensively for furniture coverings and proved to be a fabric of long-lasting quality, so that many well-preserved Georgian chairs can still be seen with their original horsehair coverings in a very good state of preservation.

Church embroidery

Very little Church embroidery appears to have been worked on canvas during the eighteenth century, but one noteworthy piece was produced by Abigail Penrose, who was responsible in 1720 for working in fine tent stitch on canvas an altar frontal for her church at Axbridge in Somerset.

---

[1] Hepplewhite: *Cabinet maker and Upholsterer's Guide*, 1788.

This one piece of canvas work is reputed to have taken her seven years to complete.

Mary Linwood and her possible influence on the decline of canvas embroidery

Towards the end of the eighteenth century the standard of embroidery design had fallen very considerably, and canvas work in particular had reached a very low ebb. The work of one outstanding woman of those days, Mary Linwood, may well have played a part in helping to bring about this decline, although her influence had been exerted unwittingly.

Mary Linwood was born in 1755 in Birmingham, and her forté was what has been called needle painting, a form of embroidery which she worked in specially-dyed crewel wools upon a material, which had likewise been woven especially for her. She became famous for this work and was greatly admired throughout her lifetime, which lasted until as late as 1845, for the production of exact copies of well-known paintings. Universal popular approval was accorded to her large, slavish copies of pictures designed by others, and some of her embroidered pictures received more admiration

than did the original paintings from which they were copied. In 1786 the Society for the Encouragement of the Arts even awarded Miss Linwood a medal for 'excellent imitation of pictures in needlework', an event which itself stresses the low level to which the art of embroidery had fallen.

Several other ladies were likewise engaged in the pursuit of picture-copying at this time, but it is noteworthy that it was Mary Linwood alone, who finally achieved great fame and the adulation of the masses, perhaps because she was somewhat of an extrovert in nature, as well as being a superb stage manager, who knew well how to arrange and display her embroideries to advantage in a permanent exhibition, which she set up at Leicester Square in London. A contemporary of hers, Miss A Lambert, in a book, which was produced in 1842, writes of Mary Linwood with fulsome praise and states: 'The aim of the accomplished needle-woman of the present day being to produce as true a picture of Nature as possible; soaring far beyond the common-place ideas of the ancient embroiderers, which perhaps are more to be admired for the richness of their materials and the labour bestowed upon them, than for any merit they possess as works of art.'

It should be noted that, although the embroidered pictures of Mary Linwood received so much

Altar frontal, 1720, worked in tent stitch on canvas
Axbridge Church, Somerset

praise during her lifetime, they were not accepted everywhere. This is evidenced by the persistent refusal of the hanging committee of the Royal Academy to accept any of her work for exhibition. It may be that Miss Linwood felt encouraged to make her copies of famous paintings, when, after the foundation of the Royal Academy in 1768, students of the Academy Schools were known to have been instructed to make copies of the work of the great masters as part of their training, although this was only done in an effort to teach them the technique of painting, and would not have been acceptable as a general practice by them. After Mary Linwood's death in 1845, when examples of her work were offered to the British Museum, they were politely refused.

When this kind of work, which is no more than the slavish copying of paintings, brings forth such an accolade of praise as was given to it at the end of the eighteenth century and during the early years of the nineteenth century, one can realise to what depths the art of embroidery had declined at that time. This is not to suggest, however, that it is wrong ever to work naturalistic scenes on canvas. Such things can be worked, provided that

the finished piece is seen to be an embroidery and does not evoke the epithet of 'just like a painting'. There is no reason whatsoever why attractive modern canvas work pictures cannot be produced to take their place beside paintings, not as rivals, but as equals. They should certainly never be worked as copies of another craft, as each craft should exploit its own technique and set forth its own special qualities without making any attempt to imitate the techniques of other crafts.

Samplers

At the end of the seventeenth century the shape of the sampler changed once more and started to become shorter in length. This tendency continued well into the first quarter of the eighteenth century until a plain, square shape eventually became the fashion, although even then variations in shape were still to be met with.

The ground material also changed slightly with the passage of time and bleached, as well as unbleached linen was in use, the texture being varied from a fine, closely-woven, even-weave linen to a coarse-mesh, linen canvas. Occasionally one comes across a sampler where the tone of the canvas used is somewhat yellow, and in a few instances a sampler may be seen, which has been worked on a material of a particularly unpleasant raw shade of yellow, almost verging on a dark mustard tone. In about 1725 it was possible to purchase a canvas made entirely of wool, which was known as tammy or samplaire. This material proved very popular for samplers, but, as wool is unfortunately a favourite food of the grub of the clothes-moth, its popularity soon faded, and by the end of the century the old style linen canvas had once more returned to favour.

Eighteenth century samplers were much more elaborate than were those of the previous era: the style of the designs had changed and become more pictorial and personal. Often a sampler would contain the picture of a house and garden, placed in an honoured position in the centre with fruit trees, birds, flowers and small animals dotted around it. Occasionally the main subject of a sampler would be the genealogical tree of the person working it.

The alphabets and numerals, which had been thought to be an essential element in samplers of the seventeenth century, now began gradually to be

Sampler, English, 1742 This sampler shows, among other motifs, an early representation of Adam and Eve and the serpent. It also includes 'boxers', but here they are fully clothed

Sampler by Mary Postle, 1747   An attractive sampler with a wide floral border, which dominates the small centre panel. Typical of the period is the verse, worked in the centre:

> Great God Compassionate and mild
>> Forgive the follies of a Child
> Teach me to pray and mind thy word
>> That I may learn to fear the Lord

omitted. Sometimes they were replaced by verses of various kinds, prayers, creeds and supplications. Such verses were at first enclosed in a very modest border edging, which soon became much wider and finally, in about 1742, became a completely decorative border, enclosing the inscriptions.

Two examples of verses on early eighteenth century samplers are the following:

> If you know Christ, you need know little more,
> if not Alls lost that you have LaRnt before.
>> Elizabeth Bayles, 1703.

> Favour is disceitful And beauty vain But
> a woman that feareth the Lord She shall be
> praised.
>> Mary Gardner, aged 9, 1740.

The growing popularity of Methodism had a profound influence on the choice of verses worked by the embroiderers of samplers in the early years of the eighteenth century. Miserable and doom-laden, but sometimes uplifting verses were handed out to the very young child to work, verses such as, 'when I am dead and laid in grave and all my bones are rotten, By this I may remembered be, when I should be forgotten.'

A large number of the inscriptions were taken from Dr Isaac Watts' *Divine and Moral Songs for Children*, which was published in 1720. John Wesley, who became a leader of the Methodist Movement, published collections of hymns between 1737 and 1786, and Philip Doddridge, another nonconformist, was also a publisher of hymns. Quotations from both men's publications were greatly used in the working of samplers.

Death and the prospect of the life hereafter appear to have been one of the main interests of the people of the late eighteenth century, and

Sampler, probably Scottish, eighteenth century, worked in silk on coarse canvas. It is the ornate lettering on this sampler which points to a Scottish origin. The date is thought to be about 1730, and it is an early example of a bordered sampler, as well as being one of the first to be decorated with a row of crowns and coronets, which have initials underneath them to indicate the various ranks of nobility: king, duke, marquis, earl, viscount, lord, count and baron

Three sketches of details from nineteenth century American Samplers Many of the American samplers contained charming little landscapes, as well as the name of the worker and the date, and most of them were surrounded by a border of flowers. All of these sketches show the weeping willow tree, which was a popular feature of many American mourning samplers

verses, such as the following, appealed to them greatly:

> Let not the morrow your vain thought employ,
> But think this Day the last you shall enjoy.

These were the moral verses young children were encouraged to work, but by far the most popular inscriptions were the Creed, the Lord's Prayer and, perhaps the most popular, the Ten Commandments. Now and again one comes across a sampler with a favourite psalm or a whole chapter from the Bible.

Another feature of the samplers of the eighteenth century was the increased use upon them of a row of crowns and coronets, such as had first appeared on samplers at the end of the seventeenth century. The popularity of this feature remained for many years and only disappeared gradually, an occasional one still being included until the year 1804. The probable reason for the inclusion of this feature on samplers at this time was the great increase in the number of titled people, who would consider it a necessity to have their stock of household linen marked with the appropriate crown or coronet associated with their family.

The end of the eighteenth century shows a distinct decline in the standard of technique in embroidery of all kinds, and the sampler was no exception to this general decline: it now became a mere vehicle for the display of the religious and moral teachings of the time.

Mention should also be made here of the fact that during the last thirty years or so of the eighteenth century it became popular to work maps on fine linen canvas, and that these pieces are often regarded as another type of sampler. They were not, however, made to serve the original purpose of a sampler, which was to provide people with examples of the best method of working certain things they would require to reproduce in embroidery later. It may have been thought at the time that embroidering a map of England or of the continent of Europe was a splendid way for small girls to learn the geography of their country, in the same way as in the previous century the samplers they had worked with alphabets and numerals, which they would use in later life to mark household linen, might well have helped in teaching the children to read and write and do figures.

Eighteenth century samplers in America

After the War of Independence in America the people naturally became very patriotic, and this is reflected in the contemporary samplers. The American Eagle and other patriotic symbols were freely used on samplers, but the basic English formula was still retained: the alphabet and numerals were still worked, and various inscriptions were included, as well as the name of the worker and the date, together with little scenes of a house and trees, surrounded by a border. That an English quality was thus retained is not altogether surprising, considering that a large proportion of the embroidery teachers in America in those days came from England, which was the home of the sampler.

One such teacher by the name of Condy came from London. Soon after her arrival in America she inserted an advertisement in the Boston News-letter of May 4th, 1738, which stated that she had for sale 'all sorts of beautiful Figures on Canvas for Tent stick' (stitch). Instead of people importing very expensive painted canvases direct from London, she suggested that she could supply them with a much cheaper version by painting the canvases herself.

The American samplers of this time were generally worked on unbleached homespun linen,

American sampler, signed and dated Lucy Potter, 1791. This sampler with its attractive border of fruit and flowers shows a distinct similarity to that of Mary Postle, dated 1747. The difference is in a wider use on this sampler of stitches such as rococo, and the fact that the border has a worked background Art Institute of Chicago

or on a mixture of wool and flax, which resulted in a rather coarse, rough fabric. Silk and linen were the main threads used for the embroidery, wool being hardly ever employed in working these samplers.

Gardens

The eighteenth century saw an ever-growing interest in gardens, and this interest is reflected in designs used for embroidery at that time. All down the ages people in this country had been intensely interested in growing things, and in the time of Queen Elizabeth I and the Stuart monarchs new plants and trees had been brought into the land from all parts of the then known world, and elaborate gardens were established with flowers carefully planted in rectangular-shaped beds, surrounded by low box and lavender hedges.

American sampler, signed and dated Catherine Ann Speel, 1805. The borders at the top and bottom of this sampler are in the form of a count-stitch pattern of tulips and carnations, whilst its much narrower side borders consist of a small running stitch-pattern *Whitman Sampler Collection, Philadelphia Museum of Art*

The more formal style of Dutch garden, which came into fashion here during the reign of William and Mary, lasted until the end of Queen Anne's reign. The cultivation of orange trees had reached a very high level in Holland, and many orangeries were built for these new gardens in England. The art of topiary, which had already been popular here for a long time, was further developed under the Dutch influence, and the English gardens became very over-crowded with these elaborately shaped trees. Another feature of the Dutch influence was provided by the numerous leaden statues, which adorned the garden walks, and among the flowers, which made the gardens gay, were masses of tulips, imported from Holland.

In 1734, during the reign of George II, Robert Furber published a book called *The Flower Garden*, which provided as many as four hundred designs, based on the gardens of his day, and a short time later a similar book was issued by Heckel. These garden books were extremely popular, not only with gardeners, but also with other craftsmen and particularly with the embroiderers, who used the designs in producing canvas work hangings and pictures.

During the reign of George III a more formal, French style of garden was introduced, where symmetry was the main theme, and small, low-growing flowers were set in their own 'parterre' and surrounded by stone or coloured boards

Sketch of a detail from an early eighteenth century tent-stitch panel A gardener with an orange tree

Stoke Edith Panel of the Tea Party This is the smaller of two large tent-stitch panels, thought to have been worked between 1730 and 1750, which formerly decorated the state bedroom at Stoke Edith in Herefordshire, and are now at Montacute House in Somerset, Stoke Edith House having been destroyed by fire in 1927. It has been suggested that the five successive wives of Thomas Foley of Stoke Edith worked these panels, but it is far more likely that they are the work of professional embroiderers. The two hangings show a formal English garden of the time of William and Mary with its lead statues, its orange treees, its tulip beds and its clipped hedges. In the fore-ground of this smaller panel of the *Tea Party* the figure of a servant is just discernible, tripping over a step and upsetting his tray, so that its contents are spread around.

The larger panel, *The Orangery Garden*, is a copy of an engraving in Ogilby's *Virgil* (1658). It shows orange trees growing in large Chinese porcelain vases, which are unusual in having been worked in chain stitch on linen and then applied on to the canvas *National Trust*

instead of the hedges of box or privet of former days. Later on these formal gardens gave way to much more open designs. Lawns were now the gardeners' favourite item, and they ran right up to the horse and stretched away to the perimeter of the garden. Extravagant designs of landscaping with large, artificial lakes and clumps of trees, planted to give the maximum natural effect, were carefully planned by eminent garden experts, such as Capability Brown. All this is reflected in the embroideries of the time.

The reign of George III and the Regency period

This period of our history, which started so promisingly for the king himself in 1760, but ended in 1820 after such a tragic decline on his side, was for the country as a whole a time of increasing wealth and leisure. The very wealthy English families suffered very little from our wars overseas at this time: even the disastrous war of the American Independence had little, if any, effect on our aristocracy, and only the lower classes and the trading fraternity suffered in the troubled times of the twenty-years war with France from 1793 to 1815. The landed gentry were happier and more prosperous than they had ever been before, and they became ever more deeply engrossed in the life they now enjoyed in their magnificent country houses, the furnishing of which, as well as the developing of their fashionable gardens, occupied their attention very considerably. They relied implicitly on the Navy to protect them from all dangers from the outside world. It was the age of the dandy, a time of extravagant living and crazy eccentricities, which culminated in the era of Beau Brummell.

This was also a time when the art of landscape painting flourished and English poets thrived. Unfortunately, however, the same cannot be said of the art of embroidery, nor of canvas work in particular, and the downward trend, which had been so clearly observed at the end of the eighteenth century, continued into the nineteenth. Pieces of canvas work, based on identical designs, are known to have existed in various parts of Britain at the end of the eighteenth century, which would appear to demonstrate that prepared kits for people to use in doing this work could already have been adopted as the generally accepted way in which amateur embroiderers might obtain suitable designs for working a canvas.

With the great increase in the wealth of the upper and middle classes, as a result of the Industrial Revolution, which had started by the beginning of this period in our history, and continued throughout it, attitudes to life were changing. The country gentleman was coming more and more into contact with life in the town, and it was considered a necessary status symbol for the young ladies of his family to be taught by a governess and later to graduate to the genteel pursuits of the drawing room. On no account were they expected to demean themselves by doing domestic tasks, but they would be taught to play the piano and sing, to paint pretty little landscapes in water colours, to read poetry and to embroider — in other words, to lead what many people today might call completely useless lives! There were, of course, some exceptions, which occurred mainly among the women members of the great political families, some of whom found more than enough work to interest them fully.

It was a very snobbish society in those days, in which the lower middle class women were endeavouring to ape their upper middle class sisters, who were themselves always trying to imitate those lucky ones in the group just above them. Thus it was that the art of embroidery, which in the past had always remained the exclusive pastime of the aristocracy and upper middle class, now gradually percolated down to the lower middle class strata of society, to the wives and daughters of wealthy farmers and rich members of the new industrial society, who, unfortunately, had little or no knowledge of the art of embroidery, and no acquaintance with the fine work of the past.

In this way centuries of lovely embroidery came to an end. Embroidery, as we have already seen, has always had its high peaks all down the ages, the period of the *Opus Anglicanum* in the fourteenth century having been a particularly

Sketch of the Servant Falling in the foreground of the Stoke Edith Panel of the Tea Party

Tent-stitch picture of the eighteenth century This
piece is worked in silk on woollen canvas and bears
the initials E H for Elizabeth Haines
Victoria and Albert Museum, London

Late eighteenth century Fragment, probably English
A canvas-work fragment, framed as a picture, showing St Cecilia at the organ. The flesh is worked in silk in straight stitches, and the draperies are in tent stitch. The background consists of couched gold threads. This small picture may have been part of the border of a larger panel *Courtesy of Patricia Anderson*

high point, but it has proved impossible to maintain this level of achievement for long, and the standard has then gradually sunk down again, as happened in the fifteenth century. The sixteenth century saw the rise of a very different form of embroidery, which again reached a peak in the reign of Elizabeth I, where it remained for about fifty years before declining once more. In the seventeenth century magnificant furnishings, which included many splendid wing chairs, provided another smaller peak of perfection before the long, slow decline which followed, and which was broken only by the production of some wonderful canvas work floor carpets during the eighteenth century.

Another element in the story of canvas work in the early years of the nineteenth century was something which was to change the very nature of this craft. It resulted from the introduction of a new type of embroidery wool, which was imported into this country from Germany, a very soft-textured wool, called Zephyr, which was produced in Gotha and then sent to Berlin to be dyed in bright, clear colours. This wool became known in Britain as Berlin wool, and the canvas work which was produced with it was called Berlin Wool Work, a name which was eventually applied to all canvas work being done in this country during the remainder of the nineteenth century.

Not only did the wool for this work come in from Germany, but designs came too, which were used to encourage the sale of the wool. These designs were in the form of charts, which were very expensive and only came into this country in small quantities at first. The patterns on the charts were printed on paper over a squared grid of lines, and were then coloured by hand. The idea was that the squares formed by the grid would match the square mesh of the canvas. The new wools, which came with the charts, had been dyed to match the colours painted on the latter, so that all that was required of the worker was to count the coloured squares on a particular chart and then work the correct number of stitches on the canvas with wool of the same colour either in tent stitch or cross stitch. In addition to the wool and the charted designs, Berlin canvas was also supplied,

This Square shows a horse and rider. It is worked on fine linen canvas, and the stitches used include satin stitch, stem stitch and tent stitch

The first of three Chinese or Korean Mandarin Squares, worked in tent stitch on silk gauze or fine linen canvas, which were produced during the nineteenth century. Such squares were originally worn in the early Ming Dynasty (AD 1368-1644), when they were used to indicate the various ranks of civil and military officials, and were very highly esteemed by those who were qualified to wear them. In those early days Mandarin Squares, which carried designs of birds, were used exclusively to denote civil officials, and those with designs of animals were kept for the military. The particular nineteenth century Mandarin Squares illustrated here show a complete departure from the earlier rigid system of applying certain designs exlusively to certain ranks and types of official. This panel has an exotic bird on a background of an all-over geometric pattern, based on the swastika

Early nineteenth century sampler, worked by Margaret Duffus in 1809   *Victoria and Albert Museum, London*

This square has a design of trees with a stylised foreground and a background based on a swastika pattern. It is worked in tent stitch, stem stitch and satin stitch, with some french knots

109

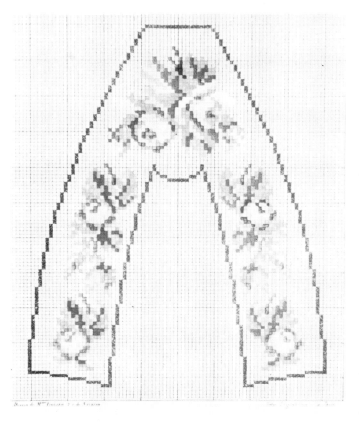

CHILD'S SLIPPER IN BERLIN WOOLWORK
EXPRESSLY DESIGNED AND PAINTED BY HAND FOR THE
'ENGLISHWOMAN'S DOMESTIC MAGAZINE'

An attractive rose pattern, drawn by Mme Figuier of Paris, to be worked in Berlin Wool

which, when it first came in, was of a very fine mesh and was made of silk upon a cotton core. It was produced in a variety of colours, including a pale shade of purple, primrose, grey and also white and black. This fine silk canvas was sufficiently attractive for the background sometimes to be left unworked, a practice which provided an added bonus by cutting down on the amount of work that was needed. Often the designs upon this silk canvas were already partly worked when bought.

At first Berlin Wool Work interested only a few of the wealthy ladies in this country. It was considered something new and different to work, and it was reasonably quick and easy to do, needing very little thought in the process. The very early Berlin prints were small and sometimes they were worked in silk instead of the Berlin wool, and

sometimes even fine, glass beads were used. These pieces of work show bunches of flowers, such as roses, auriculas and poppies, with sprays of smaller flowers among them. The floral designs at this early period of the nineteenth century were generally worked on a light fawn or beige background.

As the nineteenth century progressed, the amount of canvas work being produced very greatly increased, until it reached a point where the production rivalled that of any other period in its history. There was, however, no improvement in the standard of design. We have the Countess of Wilton, who wrote the first book on *The Art of Needlework* in 1840, to thank for a contemporary view of the work of that time. She states in her book the following: 'Of the fourteen thousand Berlin patterns which have been published, scarcely one half are moderately good; and all the best which they have produced latterly are copied from English and French prints. Contemplating the improvement that will probably ere long take place in these patterns, needlework may be said to be yet in its infancy. The improvement, however, must not be confined to the Berlin designs: the taste of the consumer, the public taste must also advance before needlework shall assume that approximation to art which is so desirable, and not perhaps now, with modern facilities, difficult of attainment.'

Thus we see that even at that time some people were critical of Berlin Wool Work. We also learn from the Countess of Wilton that 'about the year 1804-5 a print-seller in Berlin, named Philipson, published the first coloured design, on checked paper, for needlework'. Prints on squared paper had been known prior to this date, but they were solely in black and white. This easy access to a hand-coloured, printed design enabled people to work a piece of embroidery by simply copying the design mechanically square by square on to an open-mesh canvas. This Mr Philipson appears to have produced only a few designs of this kind, and a mere handful of them entered this country. It would also appear that Mr Philipson was not particularly successful in this venture himself, but his idea was a good one commercially speaking and

French hand-screen, early nineteenth century One of a ▷ pair of hand-screens on which the main design was worked in tent stitch on a background of cream silk, which was worked in elongated cross stitch horizontally upon a fine canvas of 28 threads to the inch. Such hand-screens were used to protect the complexions of the ladies from the intense heat of open fires
Victoria and Albert Museum, London

was quickly recognised as such by others, although it did nothing to help the creativity of the embroiderer.

According to Miss A Lambert, the author of *The Handbook of Needlework*, 1842, 'we are indebted to Herr Wittich for the following facts relative to the hisory of Berlin patterns: about the year 1805 a Mr Philipson published some patterns, which, being badly executed and devoid of taste, did not meet with the encouragement he expected'. The person she mentions as Herr Wittich was a Berlin print- and book-seller, named L W Wittich, who was induced by his wife, a lady of very good taste and an accomplished needlewoman, to extend his business by printing many copies of such patterns for Berlin Wool Work. Herr Wittich's comments on the work of Philipson, mentioned by Miss Lambert, could well have been biased, but in any case, his efforts in this field certainly fared better than did those of Philipson, and he established a very successful business.

A Colour Supplement for the Young Ladies' Journal, dated July 1st, 1873 This shows coloured canvas-work patterns, beneath which is printed a list of prices at which Messrs J Bedford & Co, 186 Regent Street and 46 Goodge Street, Tottenham Court Road, London, will supply subscribers to the Young Ladies' Journal with materials of various kinds

A number of other print publishers joined in what soon became for them also something very remunerative, and between 1810 and 1840 no less than 14,000 different copperplate designs of this kind were produced, as we have already seen mentioned by the Countess of Wilton. These copperplate prints, particularly the more elaborate ones, were very expensive to produce, as experienced artists were employed to make copies of famous paintings on to squared paper. The copies thus made had then to be printed and the prints hand-coloured, in order to indicate to the worker the different shades of colour to be used. The cost of producing just one of the more intricate charts could well have been anything up to £50.

It was much later in the nineteenth century before the charts were printed in colour instead of being hand-coloured, and this naturally made the charts cheaper and more readily available, but the hand-coloured type were still being produced and sold right up to the end of the century.

Such printed patterns for embroidery were imported into England by numerous publishers of engravings, such as Ackermann, who was famed for his journal, *The Repository of Arts*, published between 1809 and 1828, but Germany was, of course, the first country to produce considerable amounts of needlework based on the new designs.

Russia, England, France, America, Sweden, Denmark and Holland soon followed, the first two countries being, after Germany, by far the largest exponents of the new style. It was, indeed, a clever scheme to mass-produce at this time coloured prints, which were capable of attracting all and sundry, and it proved particularly attractive to those new-rich young ladies in England, who had no previous knowledge of embroidery, but who had an infinite amount of patience and time on their hands. They were now able to embroider one of these very expensive, imported designs by simply counting the numbers of squares on the print and matching them to the number of threads on the canvas. It was no longer necessary to employ an experienced embroiderer to help them, as no great thought and almost no skill were required to complete a piece of work, and thus to become in the end the proud possessor of a chair seat or a stool top cover, a top for an ottoman, a fire screen or some other equally welcome piece of embroidery.

In France, on the other hand, although numbers of the Berlin patterns were imported, there were many ladies who still preferred to work according to their old-established method, from designs previously traced on to canvas, and their work, which had already attained a position of superiority in Europe during the latter part of the eighteenth century, continued to hold that position during the nineteenth century.

The French style of furnishing rooms with matching sets of furniture was now dying out in England, and a freer, more relaxed style was beginning to prevail. Odd occasional chairs, stools and settees were beginning to adorn the drawing-room of this period. It was just the thing for the lady of the house to take advantage of these new designs in order to cover a favourite chair or stool.

At first, as we have seen, the Berlin patterns entered this country in small numbers, and the quantities coming in remained small until about the year 1831, when a Mr Wilks, the owner of an important London needlework shop, situated in the new and fashionable Regent Street, sent directly to Berlin for a large consignment of these prints and all the necessary canvas and wools required for working them. This proved to be a very profitable move on his part, as he remained for many years the principal importer of Berlin patterns into this country. It is interesting to read an advertisement, which he inserted many years later in the *Illustrated London News*, dated December 14th, 1844, in which he announced the following: 'A superb assortment of wools of all kinds — plain, chine and shaded, including the four-thread Berlin wool and the Imperial light-thread or double Berlin.' He goes on to state that 'all these wools, spun especially for this house, are remarkable for their quality, and present, beyond all comparison, the largest and best assorted stock in the Kingdom. Berlin patterns and every other Article, whether of British or Foreign Manufacture, used in Decorative Needlework'.

The Victorian period

The Victorian embroiderers were extremely fortunate in having a wide choice of canvases, coming both from Germany and from France, which they could use in their canvas work. All the canvas used previously was of the single-mesh type, but from about 1835 onwards a completely new type of canvas was introduced, which was thought to facilitate the working of cross stitch in interpretations of the Berlin patterns. This new canvas was known as Penelope double-thread canvas. It is thought that the name Penelope was given to this type of canvas, because it resembled in appearance a piece of single-thread canvas after lines of cross stitch had been worked on it, drawing the threads together, and had then been unpicked again, Penelope having become famous for her habit of unpicking at night the weaving she had done during the course of the previous day. Berlin also supplied a very fine silk canvas, which was extremely expensive to buy. This canvas was woven not only in white thread, but also in an off-white shade (pearl), as well as in grey, pale purple, black and a pleasant shade of pale yellow, and it, therefore, proved very suitable for working small articles, such as handbags, note-cases, bookmarkers, needle-cases and other things of that nature, where the pattern alone would be worked, and the silk canvas was attractive enough to be left unworked as background.

French linen canvas was also expensive, but nevertheless it proved a firm favourite, as the square mesh of this canvas was accurate and very evenly woven, which made it easy for the worker to reproduce the Berlin patterns upon it. The cotton canvas, produced in Germany, which was by comparison very cheap, was unpopular with the embroiderers, because the number of warp and weft threads to the inch was uneven, and the mesh of the canvas did not exactly match the mesh of the grid on the patterns. This led to the designs becoming distorted when worked. All these canvases were sold in a wide range of mesh sizes, which ranged from a coarse type with eleven threads to one inch up to a very fine one with approximately thirty-seven threads to the inch.

Nineteenth century church embroidery

The first really strong criticism of Berlin Wool Work in this country came in the 1840s from both the Roman Catholic and the Anglican Church with their keen interest in embroidery as a part of church furnishings. In 1829 the Roman Catholic Church had been freed from the restrictions it had suffered under since the time of the Reformation, and many new church buildings were planned. This gave a wonderful opportunity to the architects of the day to use their talents in designing these new buildings, and, as a result, the great Gothic revivalist movement of the nineteenth century was born. One of the most enthusiastic supporters of this revival was the English architect, Augustus Pugin (1812-1852), who not only helped to design the House of Parliament at Westminster, but also several churches, both in this country and elsewhere in Europe. Having returned to the old styles of Gothic building, it was only natural that Pugin should also strive for a revival of mediaeval styles of church embroidery to be used in the furnishings. He saw quite plainly that the contemporary embroidery style of Berlin Wool Work was not a desirable style in which to carry out the furnishings for his new churches. His book *On the*

Victorian Sampler Berlin Wool Work showing an example ▷
of 'canvas lace' at the bottom left of centre
Victoria and Albert Museum, London

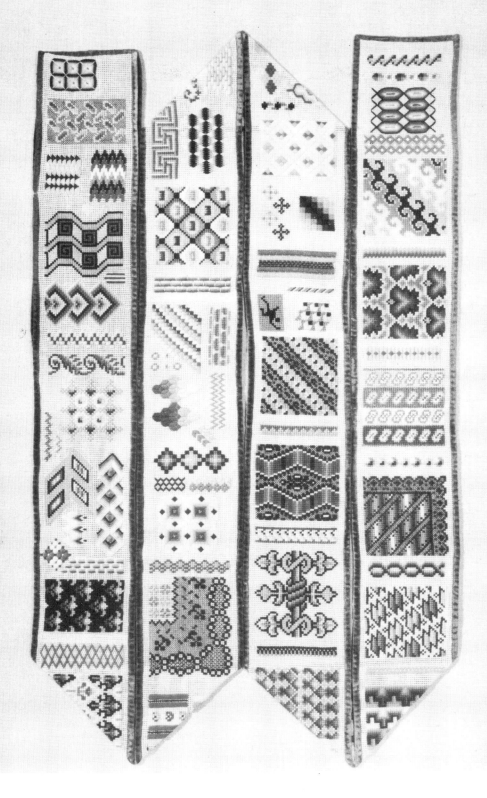

The Talisman A scene from Sir Walter Scott's novel showing the knight being presented to Berengaria inside the tent of Richard Coeur de Lion. This piece is worked in cross stitch with Berlin wools on double-mesh canvas. The faces and hands have been worked in tent stitch, which entailed splitting the canvas threads, and steel beads have been used to define the sheaths of the swords and daggers, while the dog has been worked in the soft Victorian tufting stitch. It is very difficult to give an exact date for the working of such Berlin wool work pictures, as these designs were popular over very many years *Victoria and Albert Museum, London*

Present State of Ecclesiastic Architecture in England, which was published in 1843, shows very clearly his views on the subject of church embroidery, on those things which were thought fitting and those which were not. After having soundly condemned the ladies of the day for the low level of their ecclesiastical embroideries, he earnestly impresses on all those who work for the Church, that, in seeking appropriate designs, they should adhere to *'ancient authorities*, illuminated manuscripts, stained glass and *especially brasses* (which can be easily copied by rubbing)', and he further states that these things 'will furnish excellent examples and many of them easy of imitation'. He himself designed many altar frontals, which were based on his principles, but, although many societies connected with churches were formed at about this time, in which ladies could join together to embroider altar cloths and other furnishings for the adornment of the church, very little canvas work appears to have been produced. It is quite understandable that the very thought of Berlin Wool Work in a neo-Gothic edifice was too distasteful to be considered, and, therefore, the only work which was acceptable for the purpose was silk crewel work upon figured silk damask.

Secular pieces in Victorian days

In the secular world outside the Church more and more people were becoming addicted to the new craze for Berlin Wool Work. Historical subjects were firm favourites, pictures such as Murray's 'Mary, Queen of Scots, mourning over the dying Douglas at the Battle of Langside,' and scenes from *The Talisman*, *Rob Roy* and other novels of Sir Walter Scott were greatly favoured by the masses. Perhaps the most popular of all were,

Dog on Cushion Dogs, cats, all family pets and other animals were favourite subjects for Victorian needle-workers. The dogs and the cats were generally shown seated on comfortable-looking cushions and were framed as pictures, while foxes' heads often adorned men's slippers *Victoria and Albert Museum, London*

Sketch of A prie-dieu chair (Vesper chair) as used in the ▷ home, particularly during the nineteenth century. It consisted of a low seat and a high back with a ledge on the top. Although its main purpose was for family prayers, the seat being knelt on, and the prayer book or hymn book being placed upon the ledge, it was also a good sewing chair. Many of these chairs were upholstered in Berlin wool work

however, the pictures of that great Victorian painter, Sir Edwin Landseer (1802-1873), such as his 'Bolton Abbey in the Olden Time,' 'Chevy Chase,' 'Dignity and Impudence' and 'There's Life in the Old Dog Yet,' with 'The Monarch of the Glen' as perhaps his most-worked picture ever. Landseer also painted studies of the Queen's pets, which came in for an immense amount of attention from the Victorian canvas workers. Ladies magazines were offering at this time numerous charts to

117

Panel or cushion-cover, English about 1850 A piece of canvas with the design traced upon it was placed upon the background material, and the stitches were worked through both materials. When the working was finished, the canvas threads were withdrawn to leave the worked design on the flannel background

be worked by their readers and plenty of advice on how to do so.

Equally popular for working on canvas were the floral designs, particularly those with large oriental poppies, convolvulus, the passion flower and, of course, roses and lilies, worked mostly in tent stitch. The prie-dieu chairs, which came into fashion in the 1840s, were generally covered with examples of Berlin Wool Work. This fact brought much scathing criticism from Anglian churchmen, who deplored the patterns used in covering these chairs, which were imported from abroad, as being most unsuitable. Some were covered with all-over patterns of flowers, which they thought would have been more suitable for covering chairs which would be used purely as drawing-room chairs, and others were 'sprinkled over with silly little emblems of maudlin Popery and French sentimentality boiled to rags.'[1] Even criticism such as this could not quell the enthusiasm of

---

[1] C E M, *Hints on Ornamental Needlework*, London, 1843.

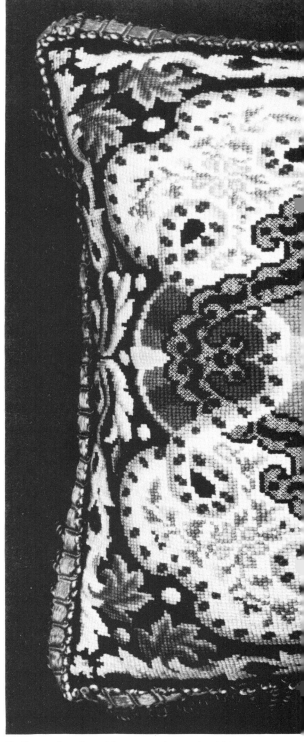

Berlin wool work cushion, approximate size 13 in. x 16½ in. (33 cm x 42 cm). This cushion was worked by Mary Anne Redfern (Mrs Hall) and has an example of Canvas Lace surrounding the central panel
Victoria and Albert Museum, London

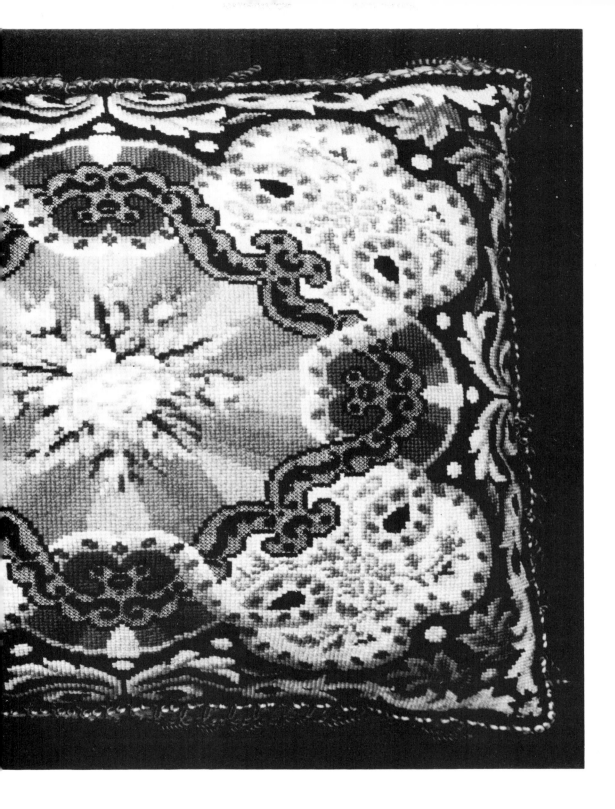

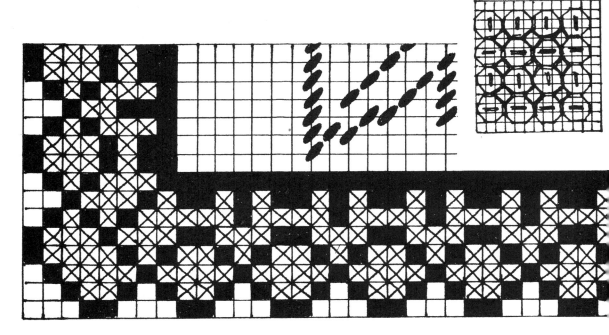

the Victorian for these charted patterns, which they found so easy to work.

At about this time also the love of the Victorians to imitate in one craft the technique of another induced them to produce a new style of canvas work. This was known as 'canvas lace', and, although it was not particularly exciting, nor very different from normal canvas work, it appealed to a number of the ladies of those days. The actual work consisted merely of surrounding parts of a design with an area of so-called 'lace', which was worked entirely in cross stitch, the most beloved of all stitches in Victorian days. The patterned part of a design was worked in a thick black silk or wool, and the imitation open net was worked with a finer black silk. It was essential to carry out the work on very fine canvas, such as 22 threads to an inch (25 cm), otherwise the effect of lace was lost.

In Miss A Lambert's book, *The Handbook of Needlework*, 1842, we are given a contemporary view of canvas lace: 'numerous patterns in imitation of lace have lately been introduced, and where judgment is used in the application of them, they certainly have some merit. The best are principally adapted for small articles; but lace and canvas work being somewhat at variance with each other, it is doubtful whether they have much claim to good taste.'

It is surprising how much the Victorians were concerned with what was or was not 'good taste'.

Two charts for working Victorian canvas lace Solid black areas are worked in black wool and the thin crosses are worked in silk. Two different methods of working are shown

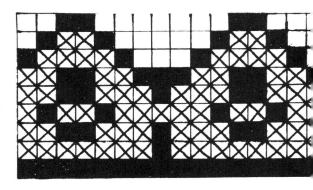

As far as canvas lace was concerned, however, the extent to which it was in good taste or not appeared to have had little effect on the opinion of the general embroidery-working public, as it proved to be a reasonably popular pursuit with them. It was new and a change from the normal Berlin Wool Work.

Crochet, which was also popular at that time, provided additional patterns ideal for use in making canvas lace, as they were available in the form of diagrams printed on squared paper in the same way as those normally used for Berlin Wool Work.

PLATE 1
Syon Cope (1300-1320)   Originally
designed as a chasuble, it was remodelled
as a cope when the heraldic orphreys
and morse were made up from parts of
other vestments
Victoria and Albert Museum, London

PLATE 2
Detail of Syon Cope, showing St Michael
overcoming the dragon
Victoria and Albert Museum, London

PLATE 3
Embroidered Orphreys, German, second half of the
fifteenth century. Six fragments from Church vestments,
showing the symbols of the Evangelists, worked with silk
and gold thread, have been applied to a linen background
Castle Museum, Berlin

PLATE 4

Orphrey of the fifteenth century An unidentified
female saint is here seen with St Peter
Victoria and Albert Museum, London

PLATE 5
The Oxburgh Panel, English, last quarter of the sixteenth
century. This piece has panels of canvas work applied to
velvet. *Victoria and Albert, Museum, London*

PLATE 6
Fruit Gathering, English, sixteenth
century. This is a cushion cover, which
has motifs worked on canvas with silk
and metal threads and applied on white
satin
Victoria and Albert Museum, London

PLATE 7

Canvas work panel, bearing the arms of Talbot, English, late sixteenth century. This panel, which is worked on canvas with silk and silver-gilt thread, has in the centre the arms of George Talbot, the Earl of Shrewsbury, fourth husband of Elizabeth of Hardwick, whose initials E S are to be seen on two of the armorial devices in the corners of the embroidery   *Hardwick Hall, National Trust*

PLATE 9
Sampler, English, first half of the seventeenth century.
This sampler is embroidered with silk and metal thread
Victoria and Albert Museum, London

PLATE 10
Berlin Woolwork, designed by L W Wittich, early nineteenth century. A hand-painted, charted design, showing a
wreath of flowers encircling an exotic bird

PLATE 8
◁ *Hatfield Carpet*, English, mid eighteenth
century. This carpet, which is owned by
The Earl Spencer, is worked in tent stitch
with wool and silk   *Hatfield House*

PLATE 11

European Architectural Heritage Year 1975 Greenwich and Chester were chosen to represent Britain at this time, and panels of embroidery were worked to mark the occasion. The Greenwich panel successfully combines motifs worked both in collage and in canvas work, which are mounted upon a background of velvet in three shades of green. The canvas-work motifs include representations of the Naval College, Eltham Palace, the Greenwich Coat-of-Arms, the Brass Foundry, Charlton House and the Cutty Sark, and the motifs in collage are of the Woolwich Town Hall, the Queen's House and Flamstead House, and the lettering and the stylised trees are also in this medium. The panel was worked by students of Maureen Bryant, who did the collage, and students of the author, who did the canvas work. The design for the whole panel was produced by the author. The Greenwich panel is now hanging in Woolwich Town Hall

PLATE 12

The Chester Panel, designed by Diana Springall. Three hundred Cheshire ladies sat down and worked for five years to produce five panels of canvas work for Chester Town Hall to celebrate the same occasion. These panels show various abstract views of Chester and were worked with wool on a 40 in. (102 cm) wide German canvas, having 12 threads to the inch (25 mm). The illustration shows the main panel and predella in position in the town hall

This kind of work was often used in the making of the many small mats upon which practically every small article, such as a lamp, a vase, a china ornament or a clock, would be placed. Such small mats were made in a variety of ways, whether it was embroidery on canvas or on silk of some description or on linen, or whether it was crochet-work, knitting or netting, and canvas lace just proved to be another suitable means of making them. It was also considered suitable for cushion covers to be provided with a border of this lace to enclose a more conventional pattern of canvas work.

Early in the nineteenth century it became popular to work small geometric patterns or stylised flowers in cross stitch on thin perforated card or Bristol board for making such articles as book-marks, notebooks or needle-cases, and homely texts and mottoes were also worked in this way to be framed and hung on the wall. This type of work may have been done mainly by children as an introduction to working on canvas. It became very popular in America, and many pieces of this work are still to be seen in the American homes of today.

Canvas work had by this time superseded crewel work, which had been the most favoured type of embroidery in America for many years, and by the 1840s the craze for Berlin Wool Work had become as great there as it was in Britain. A large quantity of hand-painted, charted designs, made especially to attract American embroiderers, were imported direct from Germany. They were based upon historical and religious scenes and pictures of happy, homely families, together with studies of flowers, birds and animals, and various patriotic motifs, and they were widely distributed over the whole of the American continent. Both naturalistic and geometric designs were exceedingly popular.

As a result there was a great outpouring in America, just as had happened here in Britain, of pieces of canvas work, both large and small. These were used not only as needlework pictures, but also as coverings for different types of furniture, such as stools, chair seats and backs, ottomans and firescreens. Small objects like pouches, bags and pocket-books were also covered in the same way with canvas embroidery. Beads were also imported in large quantities, as was the custom elsewhere in the world, and they were used with the Berlin wool in working on canvas. Sometimes a whole cushion would be worked with beads alone, but more often the beads were used simply to highlight a flower design or in working small objects, such as note cases and evening bags.

Sampler of canvas-work stitch patterns, German, early nineteenth century   *Landesgewerbemuseum, Stuttgart*

Carpets

Carpets, worked in tent stitch and cross stitch, continued to be made in the nineteenth century, but naturally, with the importation of Berlin Wool Work, the style of design changed, bringing with it a further decline both in the quality of design and of workmanship. In 1830 bleached canvas and canvas squares for this work started to come into the country, together with hand-coloured designs, printed on squared paper in the same way as those which were imported for the working of chair covers. A few years later canvases came in with the designs already traced on to them, together with the coloured wools for working and instructions on how to do so. The designs were mainly floral at first, but later this style gave way to a mixture or patchwork of designs on all sorts of subjects, including family pets, such as the sleeping cat on the mat, heads of horses and foxes, and houses, as well as wreaths or sprays of flowers.

THE BUTTERFLY LOUIS XVI CHAIR-BACK
in Berlin Wool and Silk.

THE BUTTERFLY LOUIS XVI CHAIR-SEAT
in Berlin Wool and Silk.

Hand-coloured charts for working a Victorian chair seat and chair back

The use of a number of squares of canvas for working these carpets made it very convenient for groups of people to work together on such a project, with each one working an individual square. When the required number of squares had been worked, they would be carefully joined together and a border would be worked to surround the whole carpet. A carpet, which was made in this way, measuring approximately 15 ft x 12 ft (4.5m x 3.6 m), was worked in about 1851, the year of the Great Exhibition. It has a design which is based on 63 squares, each one showing a floral pattern or a representation of a bird. The central panel of squares is surrounded by a wide border, formed from working a geometric pattern of leaves. This carpet has an accompanying plan, giving particulars of the design of each square and the name of the person who worked it. On the reverse side of the plan is the following statement: 'Description of a carpet worked by Miss Willis and her Friends and given by her to her Goddaughter Emily Ann Powell on her marriage October 28th 1851.'

Designs from bird-books — Victorian tufting

In about the year 1840 many designs were produced for the working of decorative panels and firescreens, based on the beautiful bird-books available at that time, which contained many coloured plates. The finest of these books were the two volumes of John Gould's *Birds of Australia*, which were printed in 1837-38 and 1840-48, Audubon's *Birds of America* (1827-38), which contained over four hundred plates and Edward Lear's *Illustrations of the Family of Psittacidae or Parrots* (1830-32).

The Victorian embroiderers used a new stitch, which had been introduced at this time, in working the birds' feathers in these pictures, as well as for animals' fur and flowers, and for all details of design requiring the effect of high relief. This stitch was based on herringbone stitch: a fine, tight row of herringbone stitch was worked, with subsequent rows of the same stitch of ever-increasing width worked over the top of it, until the area to be covered was completely filled. When this had been achieved, the rows of stitchery were cut through the centre, and the wool pile was clipped to the shape required. The very soft Berlin wool used in working this stitch, which is known today

Beadwork table top   This charming panel, which is 24 in. (61 cm) square, is worked entirely with fine and medium-sized beads on canvas. It shows a remarkable degree of naturalism, which is owing, no doubt, to the fact that special charts for this type of beadwork indicate to the worker the exact position and colour of each individual bead to be used. This piece was awarded a gold medal at an exhibition in Dublin. Beads for this kind of work were imported into this country from Germany and France at about the middle of the nineteenth century
Victoria and Albert Museum, London

124

Sketch of a mid-Victorian cross-stitch carpet This design shows a mixed collection of motifs, which were worked separately on canvas and then joined together to form a carpet approximately 10 ft x 7 ft (3 m x 2.1 m). The borders were worked separately

Sketch of an early Victorian chair Berlin wool work in cross, tent and tufted stitches, with a beige-coloured background

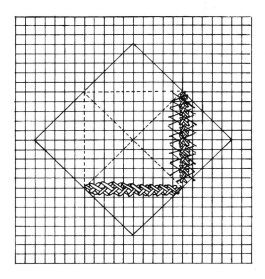

Victorian Tufting (photograph) and *diagram showing the method of working Victorian tufting* to form a small diamond shape

as Victorian tufting, plush stitch or pile stitch, gave a very tightly matted appearance to the work after it had been clipped. (See stitch diagram for the method of working).

The effects of the Industrial Revolution

The first effects of the Industrial Revolution in England had been felt at the end of the eighteenth century and during the next 50 years it brought about a complete change in the whole industrial system of the country and altered the very structure of society itself. New machinery, driven by water power, gradually replaced the tools of

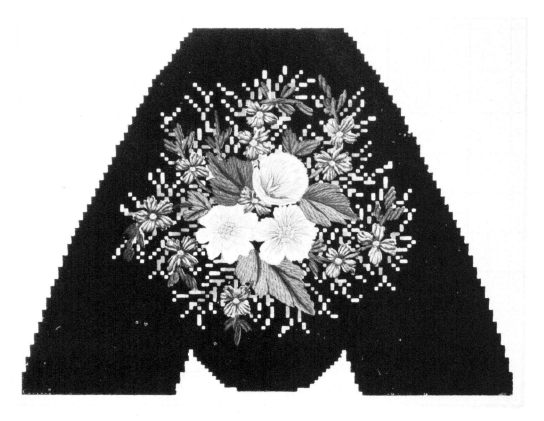

the hand-worker, and later the steam engine was introduced into the mills. The first railway came into being in the year 1823, and within the next 20 years thousands of people were able to leave their homes in villages in the country and travel by train into the towns, whilst townspeople found themselves able to explore the countryside.

From classical times onwards until the advent of the Industrial Revolution craftsmen would never allow any object they had made to leave their workshops without its having passed the highest tests of the guilds, and this applied to works of embroidery and tapestry just as stringently as to those of all other crafts. No distinction was made between the artist and the artisan, and the workshops were capable of fulfilling orders for a great variety of hand-made goods, such as glass- and silver-ware, metalwork and woodwork, including the carving of ornate picture frames, painting and sculpture, in addition to embroidery and tapestry.

The introduction of the new industrial machinery caused a break in this long tradition, and brought about the end of the many small workshops, which had supplied all the hand-made

articles of the past. The apprenticeship system also came to an end, and this led to a great decline in the standard of design, which fell to such a low level that much criticism was expressed concerning the new machine-made articles. A Parliamentary Select Committee was set up and this recommended the establishment of a School of Design, which took place in 1837 at Somerset House. Several other similar design schools were established all over the country during the next five years. Small exhibitions were held from time to time, and as early as 1847 there were signs of a revival of the decorative arts. This led a group of architects, painters and art-lovers to decide that the time was ripe for the holding of a major international exhibition in order to display to the world what had been achieved in Britain over the years, and to reveal the great triumphs of Victorian manufactory. Two of the principal instigators of this scheme were Sir Henry Cole, an art critic, who held a prominent position in the Royal Society of Arts, and Owen Jones, a designer, architect and writer. These two, together with their friends, worked hard to get the idea of an exhibition accepted. At first they met with opposition, and Parliament was dubious about the whole thing, but eventually, with tremendous support from Prince Albert, the Great Exhibition of 1851 took place in the especially built Crystal Palace in Hyde Park, London, and proved to be an enormous success, with people from all over the world flocking to see it.

The exhibition had literally something on show for everyone and was divided into sections for both professional and amateur work. The section dealing with textiles was set up in the South Central Gallery and was sub-divided into various groups, such as Woven Tapestry, Lace, Tambour Work, Embroidery and Fringes. There seem to have been separate areas for exhibiting examples of Berlin Wool Work, Needlework and other Miscellaneous Textiles. Little or no selection appears to have been made between various exhibits, as there were no less than six entries

Design for a lamp mat to be worked with Berlin wool and beads. This piece was 'expressly designed for the Englishwoman's Domestic Magazine' by Mesdames Le Boutillier, 125 Oxford Street, W

Design for a sofa cushion   to be worked in flat or button-hole stitches on canvas with Berlin wool. This was another design expressly drawn for the Englishwoman's Domestic Magazine

The Poppy Wreath Sofa cushion design   The diamond shapes placed beneath the design denote the range of shades of wool or silk to be used

AD. GOUBAUD, à Paris.

A Berlin wool and bead banner-screen produced by
A D Gaubaud, Paris

listed in the catalogues, which were in the form of
needlework pictures based on Leonardo da Vinci's
'The Last Supper', five of which were worked in
Berlin wool, and the remaining one in floss silk.
These pieces came from various parts of the country
and one of them, which is signed 'Mrs J Morris fecit
1851', is still to be seen in the Victorian and
Albert Museum, London. Another one, which
came from Oxford, was said to have contained
500,000 stitches. There were also four Berlin Wool
Work pieces depicting 'Mary, Queen of Scots,
mourning over the dying Douglas at the Battle of
Langside'. These four entries were the work of
ladies living in the Southern part of England and
not, as might have been expected, of ladies living
North of the border.

Carpets and rugs, worked in thick Berlin wools

on a coarse type of canvas, were also on display. Most of these were worked by a number of friends or groups of people working on a co-operative basis, in the same way as we have already noticed in the case of a carpet worked by Miss Willis and her Friends. One outstanding example called the 'Ladies' Carpet', which was made for presentation to Queen Victoria, had been specially designed by the architect, J W Papworth. It was constructed in the manner usually adopted for the working of these hand-made canvas work carpets, being divided into 152 squares, with one square for each lady participating in the project. When the work was finished, the squares, which were filled with small floral and geometric patterns, were carefully joined together to form the central area of the carpet and were then surrounded with an heraldic border, which included the initials of all the ladies involved in the working. The present whereabouts of this carpet are unknown, and it would appear to have disappeared completely, without even an illustration of it being available to us. Another smaller carpet of the same kind, which was made up of a group of 13 squares in length and seven in width, and which was reputed to have been the work of a group of Irish ladies, has also been lost without trace. Each of the squares forming this carpet was said to show a wide variety of designs, such as flowers, birds, fruit and landscapes.

The Last Supper by Leonardo da Vinci   Many copies of this famous painting were carried out in needlework over a period of several years, and no less than six Berlin Wool Work pictures were shown at the Great Exhibition in 1851. Even today it is possible to buy painted canvases of this picture to work
Victoria and Albert Museum, London

Efforts to improve design generally in the nineteenth century

Although the Great Exhibition of 1851 proved a financial success beyond all expectations, it came as a terrible shock to its organisers to see how low was the standard of British decorative design as compared with the rest of Europe, with the exception of Belgium, which had an equally low standard. Sir Henry Cole and Owen Jones, who had been heavily involved in organising the exhibition, became intensely dissatisfied with the English exhibits, being particularly worried at the low standard of design of the machine-made articles with their excessive amount of ornamentation as compared with the continental entries. While accepting the fact that the age of the machine had arrived, and that machine-made articles were here to stay, they felt that, if well-known painters and sculptors could be persuaded

to become industrial designers, things would improve. The financial success of the Great Exhibition enabled Sir Henry Cole to become engaged in a variety of successful public projects, and he bore the major share in founding, and was for many years in charge of what eventually became the Victoria and Albert Museum and the Science Museum.

One year after holding the Great Exhibition the British government established the Museum of Manufacturers in Marlborough House in order to accommodate a collection of examples of the decorative arts, which had been displayed at the Exhibition, together with some similar articles from the Government School of Design, which had been renamed the Museum of Ornamental Art at the time of the Great Exhibition. It was this collection of objects which formed the basis of the Victoria and Albert Museum, for the present building of which in South Kensington Queen Victoria laid the corner stone in 1899. The official opening of the museum was performed by King Edward VII in 1909. The Government School of Design was also moved to South Kensington. This happened in the year 1897, and the School became known as the Royal College of Art.

William Morris

During the second half of the nineteenth century William Morris did much to improve design, but, unlike Sir Henry Cole, he was against the idea that well-known artists should be involved with the designing of machine-made articles. He was, in fact, a keen advocate of getting back to the production of articles by hand, and here he thought at first that 'the hand that made the article should be the same hand which had designed it'. In the course of time, however, he came to realise that this ideal was impossible of attainment, and in a very short while we find him producing many designs not only for stained glass and wall paper, but also for embroideries, which other people were to work. It has to be admitted, however, that he did little to help improve canvas work designs, and it would appear that embroidery on canvas, being slow to work and having rigid rules, did not appeal to his temperament. He felt that it was too restrictive and so preferred a freer and more fluid medium. His designs were large and flowing, many of them being based upon early Italian cut velvets. The soft, fluffy Berlin wools, with their strident colouring, heartily sickened him, and he aimed to get back to a method of dyeing with the natural dyestuffs and thus back to beautiful shades, where the colours blended softly and pleasantly together with no danger of clashing.

When we look today at the designs of William Morris, we can see how very suitable they would have been, if carried out on canvas. Most of his embroidery designs for things like altar frontals were intended to be worked in silk and gold upon a silk foundation, while many others of a coarser nature were worked in wool on coarse linen. There is, however, one altar frontal designed by him, which is worked on canvas and can be seen in Busbridge Parish Church in Godalming, Surrey. It measures 81½ in. x 37½ in. (2 m x 95 cm) and is worked in coloured silk. Many of Morris's designs were repeat patterns, intended for chintz, wall papers and large embroidered hangings, and this may explain why the design for this particular altar frontal appears not to have been drawn specifically for the purpose. One might be forgiven for believing that the original design was intended for wall paper or for a large wall hanging, and that the lower section of it has been adapted for use on this particular altar frontal.

As a direct result of the teaching of Morris and his associates, many societies were formed in order 'to promote a cultivation of Art as directly applicable to the Crafts'. One such society was known as the Art-Workers Guild and was formed in 1884, and another, which was set up four years later, was the Arts and Crafts Exhibition Society, but the one, which was of most interest to the embroiderer at this time, was, of course, the Royal School of Art Needlework.

The Royal School of Needlework

Before the Industrial Revolution the craft of embroidery had been firmly in the hands of the ladies of the upper classes, who had themselves passed on the knowledge of their craft to their children, often employing a skilled embroiderer to assist them. Later, when masses of charts for Berlin Wool Work had flooded the market, members of all classes of society were able to take

Altar frontal, designed by William Morris in the 1870s and worked with silk on canvas   *The Parish Church, Busbridge, near Godalming, Surrey*

132

up some form of embroidery. Unfortunately, however, there was now no one who could help them to improve the standard of their work or lead them on to new and better designs, no gentle mammas now, who were capable of guiding the vast numbers of new embroideresses. It was in order to help improve this situation that the Royal School of Art Needlework was founded in 1872 by a group of influential upper-class ladies. Artists such as Edward Burne-Jones, Selwyn Image, Walter Crane and William Morris gave their support to the scheme and provided many designs for the ladies to work

Other schools of embroidery, such as the Ladies Ecclesiastical Embroidery Society and the Leek Society, had been founded earlier, but, as the new school was under royal patronage, as well as having the support of the eminent artists mentioned, it started life on a very firm basis and soon became very successful. It was founded primarily as a charity to provide work for 'reduced and distressed gentlewomen' and consisted of a training school, one workroom and a showroom. The rules were very strict, and it was no easy matter to gain admission to the training school: two referees of undoubted reputation were needed to vouch for the fact that the applicant was 'a gentlewoman by birth and education' and that she was 'in every way suitable to our Association of Ladies'. A fee of nine guineas had to be paid for a course of nine lessions and was obligatory for all participants, whether they were already hightly-skilled workers in embroidery or not. After completing their nine training lessons, and if they were considered suitable workers, they were paid by the piece for the embroidery they did, the average weekly earnings amounting to thirty shillings.

It was only after the training school and work-room had become well-established, that the council considered starting non-vocational classes at the Royal School for the many ladies wishing to avail themselves of the opportunity to learn the new type of embroidery, which was in the true manner of William Morris — in other words, crewel-work. Contrary to Morris's original idea, however, that the work should be done by the same person as had designed it, the young ladies were able to purchase from the School pieces of linen upon which sprays of flowers had already been traced for working. They paid four to five shillings for these pieces according to the size. The teacher also had in her possession pieces of prepared and commenced work, which the students could purchase and upon which they could practise the various stitches. These designs would be for such small things as cushions, chair-back covers, hand screens, stool tops and bell pulls.

Most of the designs provided at this time were for crewel work in wool and silk on a linen or silk background. Canvas work appears to have been completely ignored and to have remained in the doldrums for a long time. It seems as if the earlier colossal outpouring of Berlin Wool Work had totally exhausted the embroiderers in all nations, and for many years this type of embroidery was looked on with horror and detestation. Any canvas work, which was produced in the period from the later years of the nineteenth century until the end of the first twenty years of the twentieth century, was, apart from the few dying remains of Berlin Wool Work, mainly in the form of reproductions of Queen Anne and Georgian work, used for furniture coverings.

Some ten years after its foundation the Royal School of Needlework finally became self-supporting. It not only found a market for pieces of prepared work, but its reputation had by now grown so considerably that many church architects were ready to place orders with it for works of embroidery which they required. William Morris also supplied the School with many orders, and one is left with the feeling that he benefitted greatly from this arrangement by having his designs expertly worked in readiness for sale later through his firm of Morris, Marshall, Faulkner and Co.

The real break-through, which led on to the final success of the Royal School, was the fact that in the Philadelphia Centennial Exhibition of 1876 the School had exhibited a large crewel-work project, devised by Walter Crane. This proved to be a great success, receiving the highest award in the exhibition, and America was conquered! Philadelphia already had its own School of Art Needlework, but nothing would satisfy them there until a member of staff from the Royal School was sent over from London to take charge of it for them.

The Royal School went on from success to success, and in 1899 it left its somewhat humble location in Sloane Street and moved to a new building in Exhibition Road, South Kensington, having outlived all other embroidery societies, with the exception of the Ladies Work Society. It is interesting to note that, as a result of this move to South Kensington, crewel work came to be known in America as 'South Kensington embroidery', a name for it which can still be heard there even today. The Royal School made a further move to its present location in Prince's

A print showing embroidery designs being prepared and transferred on to the material for working Venice, 1878
Victoria and Albert Museum, London

Top left
Tracing the design on to the material by the aid of a lighted candl[l]

Top right
Tracing the design on to the material by propping the frame up against the light of a window

Bottom left
Transferring a design by the 'prick and pounce' method

Bottom right
Tracing part of a design on to a fresh piece of paper

Gate in 1948.

Although the Royal School of Needlework was concerned almost completely with the production of crewel work, it did commence producing canvas work in the late twenties of this century, the designs for which were mainly replicas of old embroideries in the Victoria and Albert Museum.

The Cambridge Tapestry Company

In 1898 the Cambridge Tapestry Company was founded to deal with the repair of valuable antique embroideries and tapestries, and it functioned for forty-two years, being forced to close down in 1940 after the outbreak of war, in the same way as the Merton Abbey Works, which had been established by William Morris and his associates, had to close, as they were both regarded by the government of the day as luxury firms, unable to perform any useful work to aid the war effort.

Painted design   on French linen canvas ready for working. This is a design as produced by the Cambridge Tapestry Company

The Cambridge Tapestry Company was situated in a large house in Thompson's Lane, Cambridge, with a London showroom in Hills Place, W1. In the house in Thompson's Lane were an office and showrooms, and the work was carried out in two very large workrooms at the back of the building, one of which contained both high- and low-looms for the weaving of sections of tapestry for use in the reparation of large Gothic and seventeenth century tapestries, and the other contained embroidery frames and housed at one time some fifty or sixty work-girls with varying degrees of proficiency in embroidery. Adjoining the workroom was a small store-room, which contained a supply of wools, silks, canvas and all the other articles required in the work. A large drawing office was situated on the upper floor at the back of the house above the workroom and here the designs for the tapestry work and the embroidery were drawn up. At one time this drawing office contained from twenty-five to thirty young people, of whom I myself was one, who had come from the Local Art School to be trained in designing for all types of embroidery and woven tapestry.

Painted design for a stool top on Penelope canvas. This
design was based on a woven tapestry border

Painted design for a chair seat   on double-thread canvas.
The design was adapted from an eighteenth century chair-
seat

The hierarchy of the drawing office consisted of three Associates of the Royal College of Art, who were in charge of the training of the young people, and there were several other fully-trained designers. The actual number employed naturally varied' from time to time, as people came and went.

At first the firm dealt solely with the principal antique dealers throughout the country, and many pieces of old embroidery, such as Elizabethan hangings, Stuart pictures and Jacobean curtains, as well as pieces of Queen Anne and Georgian work, were sent to them to be prepared or slavishly copied. Later, however, in the 1920s and 1930s the range of its work was extended, when many wealthy ladies persuaded the firm to supply them with painted canvases to enable them to work their own furnishings. The designs used for this work were at first mainly traditional and very many Queen Anne chair seats and stool tops were worked, as well as seats and backs for large settees, not to mention fire-screens. It was not only painted canvases which were in demand, but many of the ladies had their canvases partly worked as well. The wools and silks for working were put into ranges and numbered, so that they were all ready for the embroideress to use in working. Lessons in working on canvas were also given to clients, when requested.

The Cambridge Tapestry Company was little known outside the sphere of the antiques world and the higher echelons of society. It is reputed never to have advertised its work, except on two occasions: one of these was when the first number of *Embroidery*, the journal of the Embroiderers' Guild, was published in December, 1932, and the other was when an advertisement was inserted, under protest, in the local newspaper, the *Cambridge Daily News*, to mark the visit to the firm of Queen Mary to see the tapestry, which was being woven there for presentation by a number of personal friends to King George V and Queen Mary on the occasion of their Silver Jubilee in 1935. Unfortunately, the King himself never saw the tapestry, as he died before the work on it was completed. Queen Mary, however, visited the firm on several occasions over the years, and on one visit she was accompanied by the then Duchess of York, now Queen Elizabeth, the Queen Mother.

In the late 1920s people were beginning to break away from the old, traditional designs and were looking for more modern things to work. They took photographs of their large country houses and gardens, with sometimes a favourite dog or horse — all subjects which had been familiar in the seventeenth century — and requested designs based upon them. Often several small, beautifully painted sketches would be submitted for approval before an order was obtained.

When the Cambridge Tapestry Company had to close in 1940, the needlework section of the firm and the existing stock of materials were acquired by the Royal School of Needlework, which was able to remain operational during the war, because, unlike the Cambridge firm, it was registered as a charitable organisation. To its workers was given the war-time task of embroidering badges for the Army, the Royal Navy and the Royal Air Force. The Royal School was thus able to come through the war-time difficulties and continue functioning to this day as one of the longest-running schools of embroidery in England. All the highly-skilled needlewomen of the Cambridge Tapestry Company were directed by the Ministry of Labour to other more important war-work. Many were obliged to go, as were the less-skilled workers, into the local factories, making jam, radios and scientific instruments, while others found more congenial work where they could. The design staff were scattered throughout the country, with some of them working at least for a while with the Royal School of Needlework. Having the work-force dissipated in this way proved to be a castastrophe from which a firm of this nature could not recover.

The Embroiderers' Guild

Although the Royal School of Needlework was founded as a charity to help 'reduced and distressed gentlewomen', its members very soon decided to enlarge their horizons and accept others who had been trained to become teachers in technical and secondary schools. Subsequently a number of past students of the Royal School decided to get together and form a society of their own to be known as the Society of Certificated Embroideresses, which would restrict its membership to those holding a teacher's diploma and a certificate showing a two years attendance at the Royal School. They soon found, however, that this was an unacceptable restriction on their membership and decided to admit other members without these qualifications, as long as they were satisfied that their standard of work was good enough. In the year 1920 this society became known as the Embroiderers' Guild.

Summing up the Victorian era

In spite of the tremendous criticism which has been levied against the Victorian embroiderers

Reverse side of the tent-stitch handbag

A small tent-stitch handbag, worked on fine, yellow, French canvas with wool and silk. The design was adapted from a seventeenth century picture. The front of the bag is unfinished. It has a few bullion stitches adorning the centre of the rose

A reproduction of a Queen Anne dining-room chair seat This was one of a set of six, worked in tent stitch on 18 mesh French linen canvas. They were worked with wool and silk, and have a pale blue silk background to the centre panel. The outer background is worked with five shades of maroon-coloured wool

both in their own day and since, their work should not be dismissed as entirely without merit. In an age when mechanical invention and technical advancement reigned supreme, it could hardly be expected that so unimportant an art as embroidery, which, after all, was almost universally regarded at that time as 'just woman's work', would receive much attention from good, qualified designers. The well-organised importation of Berlin wools and designs into this country from Germany must have totally swamped any desire on the part of our native designers to compete, even if such a desire had existed in the first place.

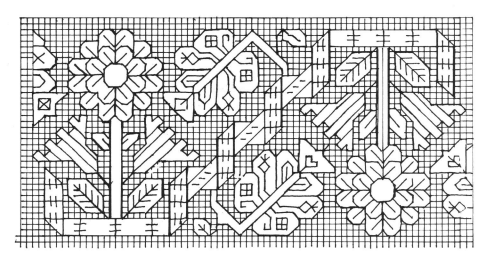

Two sketches of repeat designs, adapted from a seven-teenth century sampler This was the type of design which was used by Louisa Pesel for the production of church kneelers in the 1930s

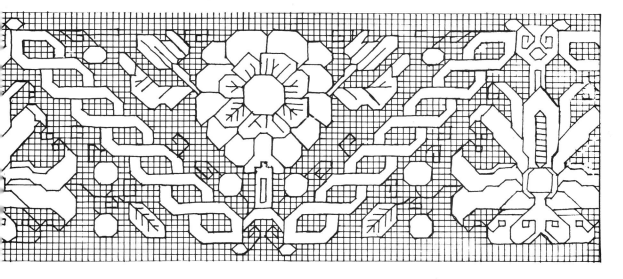

The actual amount of work produced by the Victorian ladies was very great indeed, and it consisted not only of Berlin Wool Work, which was, of course, produced in large quantities, but also of many examples of other allied embroidery techniques, such as crochet, tatting, crewel work, broderie anglaise, goldwork, drawn thread work, patchwork and quilting, which were brought to a very high level of perfection. Samplers

◁ *Two bead evening bags* The top one is English of the late nineteenth century or the early twentieth century. The bottom one is French of the 1930s

also continued to be worked throughout the nineteenth century. At first they were based on designs similar to those used in the eighteenth century, but later they became a means of recording stitches and stitch-patterns and thus reverted to their original purpose. These Victorian samplers were generally worked on double-thread (Penelope) canvas with Berlin wool. Whatever else the Victorian ladies did, or did not do, they at least kept the art of handwork very much alive, which was a major achievement when performed against a background of the ever-increasing power of the machine.

The twentieth century

One of a set of kneelers produced in 1929   These kneelers were worked by the Wolvesey Canvas Embroidery Guild for the Bishop of Winchester's Private Chapel at Wolvesey. This is the earliest known kneeler project. The designs were adapted and the work directed by Louisa F Pesel. The work was carried out on hemp canvas with wool in long-legged cross stitch

There were many keen embroiderers, whose work bridged the years from Victorian days to the early years of the present century. One of these was Louisa Frances Pesel (1870-1947). She had taken a keen interest in embroidery for many years and had assisted W G Paulson Townsend with his book, *Embroidery or the Craft of the Needle*, which was published in 1899. This book does not, however,

include any reference to canvas work, which only goes to show the depths to which this form of embroidery had sunk at that time. Louisa Pesel had studied drawing and design with Lewis F. Day, and on his recommendation she was appointed to be in charge of the Royal Hellenic Schools of Embroidery and Laces in Athens. This appointment lasted from 1903 to 1907, when she returned to this country. In the following year she was elected to be a member of the Society of Certificated Embroideresses and later, in the year 1920, when the Society changed its name to the Embroiderers' Guild, she became its president, an appointment which lasted for two years.

In 1931 Louisa Pesel was approached by the Dean and Chapter of Winchester Cathedral and asked to initiate work for the production of a number of kneelers (hassocks), long cushions and almsbags, which were to be covered with canvas work. She accepted the task and arranged for a number of people to get together and work the

patterns she had designed. Louisa Pesel had a fine, inborn sense of colour and had acquired a sound knowledge of stitchery. Her designs, however, were far from original, being based largely on the seventeenth and eighteenth century samplers, which she had studied in the Victoria and Albert Museum. She relied on her friend, Sybil Blunt, a painter, to supply the historical features which were needed, while she herself designed the count-stitch patterns which surrounded them. These latter were worked mainly in long-legged cross,

One of a series of 132 kneelers, which were worked in 1969 to celebrate the centenary of Girton College, Cambridge. The designs were by Jennifer Gray, working in conjunction with Mrs Michael Kitson, and are based mainly on mosaics and low relief carvings in Ravenna and Rome. They are worked on 18-mesh, single-thread canvas with Anchor Tápisserie wool and coton perlé No. 5. The subject of this particular kneeler is a Gold-finch triumphing over the Crown of Thorns, which symbolizes the Crucifixion

cross, tent rice and satin stitches and, when completed, they proved to be very attractive. The whole project took two hundred ardent workers just five years to complete.

This initial move on the part of Winchester Cathedral, to replace their existing kneelers with some others, which had more attractive coverings, started a desire for many other churches to follow this idea and replace old hassocks, which were often covered with such things as leatherette, rush or perhaps a hardwearing material like baize or serge, with new ones having much more attractive coverings, worked on canvas. It was not until after the second world war, however, that this idea inspired by Winchester really got going.

There were many keen teachers, whose enthu-siasm had kept the spirit of embroidery alive during the war years, and they were the people whose influence led on to the further development of such church work in various parts of this country after the war. Many sets of canvas work kneelers were produced with designs from various sources, and several of them were quite naturally worked for memorial purposes, one such set being the kneelers for Saint Clement Danes in the Strand, London, the Royal Air Force Church. Guildford Cathedral was also provided with a very attractive set, which was worked in shades of blue and fawn, and Coventry Cathedral acquired a set of kneelers, based upon designs provided by the architect, Sir Basil Spence, which reflected in their colouring the beauty of the magnificent baptistry windows

The Oasis by Claude Flight, 1920s-1930s This is worked entirely in cross stitch with wool, and there is no attempt at shading. All Claude Flight's designs were geometric and were carefully planned in great detail before working

Claude Flight, well known in his own day as a designer, was intrigued by the use of geometric designs for embroidery. The textural quality of the stitches used made no impact on him whatsoever, and one wonders why he chose such a time-consuming type of embroidery as canvas work for carrying out his designs, when it is reported that he himself said, 'that in the ideal most of his designs could be carried out as effectively by machine as by the embroiderer, so little are they dependent upon hand-work *Eleanor French*, writing in *Embroidery* in 1935

Lupins by Claude Flight, 1920s-1930s This piece is worked on canvas with coloured wools in cross stitch

◁ *A cushion*, which was designed by Claude Flight in the 1930s, shows the figure of a squatting Indian. It is worked on canvas with wool in cross stitch.

of the new cathedral. Manchester Cathedral is yet another church building which received a delightful set of kneelers, worked since the war upon canvas in many different stitches and in lovely, lively colouring, which is so right for the dark interior of the building.

The development of design in modern canvas embroidery

Attitudes towards design for embroidery have changed very considerably from what was thought desirable in the early years of this century to what is acceptable practice today. Previously no great emphasis was placed upon persuading students to draw up their own designs, and keen teachers of embroidery, who opposed the idea of their students' following the popular habit of working designs, which were based on transfers, or of using commercially painted canvases, nevertheless went no further than the producing of designs of their own for students to work under their instruction.

In the years between the two world wars an enormous amount of new thought was given, both in the Art Schools and in teachers' training colleges, to the teaching of design as it applied to various crafts and particularly to embroidery. Many of these new ideas were based upon the teaching of the Bauhaus, an institution which had been set up in Germany in 1919 by Walter Gropius with the object of promoting greater freedom in the creative arts, and which influenced the modern movement in design for many years, even after it was disbanded in Germany on the advent of the Hitler regime in 1933. Many of its teachers then left their homeland and went to various other European countries and to America, thus spreading their ideas around the world.

This modern movement in design eventually succeeded in freeing canvas work from the restrictive rules of the Victorian age, from which it had suffered for so long, so that it now ceased to be produced simply in the form of pieces of tent stitch and cross stitch, worked in Berlin wools. The progress of the new ideas was slow at first, but gradually more and more people began to accept the change to abstract designs for embroidery. It must, however, be admitted that this new style of design was not acceptable to all, and

Lupins, a fire-screen, which was designed and worked by Marjorie Laurence in the 1940s. It is worked mainly in tent and gros point stitches

The Skaters This panel was produced by Edith Sales in about 1945. It is worked with wool in various stitches on canvas, and the design gives a fine feeling of movement on the ice

Count-stitch patterns for canvas work

147

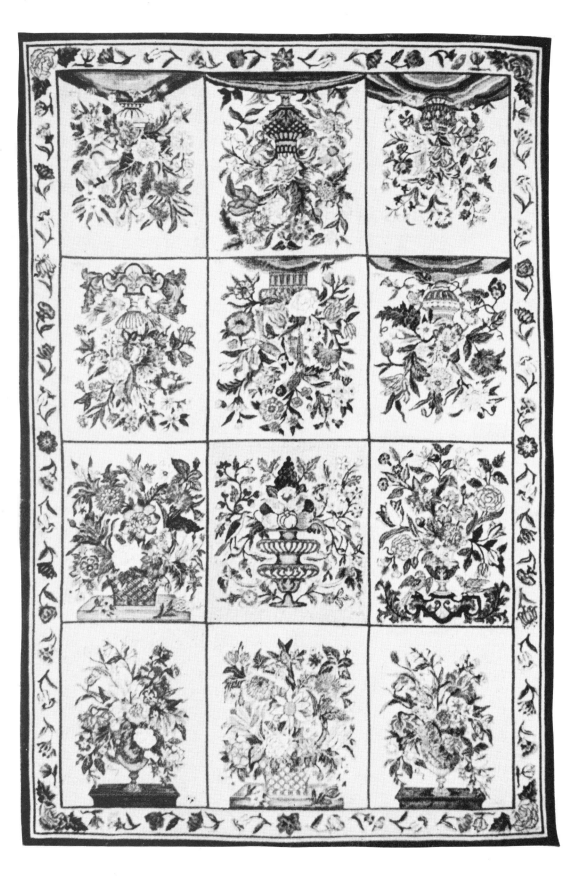

Feathers, worked by May Thurgood, 1950 A tent-stitch picture on 18-mesh canvas, this design shows a break away from the earlier, more formal treatment of colour and shading. Both silk and wool have been used for working it, and the colours used are blues, blue-greens, white and black on a shaded background of maroon

◁ *Queen Mary's Carpet, 1950* This carpet, which is 10 ft 2 in. x 6 ft 9½ in. (3.1 m x 2 m), is worked in gros point on linen canvas. It is signed 'Mary R' in the corner of each of the twelve panels. Queen Mary worked on these panels for eight years, before they were completed and assembled as a carpet in 1950. The panels were worked separately, being based on eighteenth century designs from the Victoria and Albert Museum and else-where. The canvases were prepared by the Royal School of Needlework in readiness for the queen to work. When finsished, the carpet was presented by her majesty to the nation for sale as a contribution to the dollar export drive of those days. It was bought by the Imperial Order of Daughters of the Empire in Canada for the sum of 100,000 dollars (£32,500).

Stool top, worked by Rennie Westmacott, 1954 This piece of canvas work was carried out in tent stitch with silks and vegetable-dyed wools on Penelope 9/18 mesh canvas

149

Fabulous Beasts, 1954   A canvas-work panel, worked on 18-mesh canvas in tent stitch with silk and vegetable-dyed wools. Bright pinks, grays, white and a purple range of wools have been used for the leaves and flowers in the centre of the panel, which are on a background of yellow silk. The rest of the panel is in wool with only the highlights in silk.

This design with its bright, cheerful colouring proved a great favourite and was worked as many as five or six times by different people

◁ *The Bonfire, designed by Mary Thodes and worked by Rennie Westmacott, 1956*   A small canvas-work picture, worked in tent stitch with silk and wool on Penelope (double-thread) canvas with 18/36-mesh

Fire-screen, worked by R Rogers, 1956   A panel of irises, worked on 16-mesh canvas in tent stitch, with a background of Hungarian stitch, is surrounded by a decorative archway

Chair-back, Mary Rhodes, 1958 A design of flowers and leaves, worked in tent stitch with silks and vegetable-dyed wools. The centre background is worked in several shades of blue and bluey-green, and the surround is ▽ yellow with black stars

Stool top, worked by Nellie J Old, 1956 A piece worked in tent stitch with silks and vegetable-dyed wools on Penelope canvas, having a mesh of 18/36

even today there are many who are unable to see anything of beauty in the mere grouping together of shapes and lines or the juxtaposition of interesting colours, and who still prefer to work the easily recognisable things they see around them. More and more people have, however, come to realise that beautiful effects can be obtained by using simple design shapes and lines and developing them by the introduction of texture. With the enormous number of stitches available, which are so varied in shape and size, almost any effect can be realized on canvas.

Very little, if any, serious embroidery had been undertaken during the two world wars, mainly because of the severe shortage of materials, but in the fifties and sixties, when conditions had greatly improved, the interest in canvas embroidery, which had been in evidence between the wars, showed renewed vigour, and it has continued to grow in popularity right up to the present day. Several books have been published which show how suitable designs may be produced for working on canvas, and the embroiderer is no longer dependent upon the painter for ideas. This is a new departure of which the twentieth century may be justly proud, where students are shown how they can obtain their own designs and develop them into pieces of embroidery by selecting

Tent-stitch picture, worked by L Milton, 1958 Violets,
primroses and dandelions, worked in silk and vegetable-
dyed wool on a variegated background

Mirror surround, worked by Miriam Bawden, 1960 This mirror-surround is worked in tent, cross, eyelet and Smyrna stitches, using silk, wool and lurex thread in shades of blue, bright pink and purple on a background of white

Small picture, worked by Lilian Hill, 1960s   Three figures are worked on 16-mesh canvas with silks and natural-dyed wools, which have a colouring of bright pink, orange, yellow, purple and black. The stitches used include tent, stem, mosaic and Smyrna on a background of small diagonal stitch

Canvas-work picture, worked by Lilian Hill, 1960s   A semi-abstract design, which shows a seated woman holding flowers. It is worked with vegetable-dyed wools in mosaic and small diagonal stitches, together with a few eyelets, tent and Smyrna stitches

Canvas-work panel of the period 1950-60, now in the ▷ War-Memorial Chapel at Washington Cathedral, USA. The design of this large panel, measuring 12 ft x 9 ft (3.6 m x 2.7 m) includes the seals of the fifty states and the District of Columbia, which have all been worked separately and then applied to the background. This consists of a tree with many branches, on to which the seals have been fixed by the 'tie-in' method, in which unravelled canvas threads are taken one at a time through to the back of the work and fastened off. The seals of the Army, Navy, Air Force, Coast Guard and Marines are included in the border. The panel was designed by the Needlework Studio of Byrn Mawr, Pennsylvania, and eighty-nine women took part in the working

Flower-shape fire-screen, worked by M Godley, 1962
This piece is worked in tent stitch in shades of blue and
green on a white cushion-stitch background. Both silk
and wool have been used, and silver glass bugle beads
outline the stamens

1913

158

Exotic Birds, worked by Winnie Browning, 1961   A long, narrow panel, worked in tent stitch, using silks and vegetable-dyed wools. It shows a flock of birds in bright, attractive colours against a shaded blue background

Greenwich Institute Panel, 1963   This needlework panel was designed by the author and worked on 16-mesh canvas by a number of her students at Greenwich Adult Institute, using silk and vegetable-dyed wools. It was presented by the students to Greenwich Institute on the occasion of its fiftieth anniversary. The design shows an owl holding the torch of learning, and it also contains representations of drama, music, flower-arrangement, pottery, art and the needlecrafts. The two coats-of-arms are those of Greenwich and the London County Council. The background colouring, proceeding from left to right, is orange-rust for the Autumn, green for the Spring and blue and yellow for the Summer term
Charlton House, London, SE7

Sub Aqua, worked by Vera Moth, 1963   A beautiful
canvas-work panel, which is worked with wool and silk
in tent stitch, is shown here in its unfinished state. It
demonstrates clearly an interesting method of shading
the background, when working in tent stitch, by using
two related shades of a colour, and thus avoiding a
dead flat effect. The colours used are pink, orange, blue-
greens, mauves, yellows and a sludgy green, and all the
wools used have been dyed with vegetable dyes

Detail of a panel, 1964, showing how holes were cut in
the canvas to enable coloured glass to be placed behind
the work

160

Seahorses, worked by Daisy Chamberlin, 1964   A canvas-work panel, worked in tent stitch with silk and vegetable-dyed wools

Canvas-work panel, worked by Betty Searle, 1964   This floral design is worked on Penelope canvas in tent stitch on a blue cross-stitch background

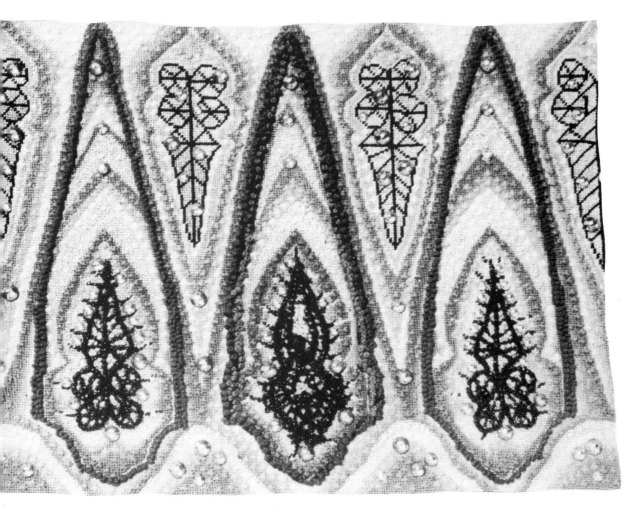

Cover for a table-lamp base, worked by Lilian Hill, 1965   This was the first piece made for this pupose, and it is seen here prior to being mounted

suitable colour schemes and a wide variety of stitches.

Many people are availing themselves of this opportunity to produce their own designs, and some very attractive things are being done, involving a great deal of experimental work. We may not like everything we see being done in the world of embroidery, but, if this form of art is to survive and have a good future, it must, like any other, be open to development and constant change. It cannot stand still or go into reverse, otherwise it will die. Both the nature of the designs used, and the method of working which is adopted, should reflect the society of our day, and should not necessarily be in the form which most appeals to

us personally. We have certainly come a very long way since that time in the 1920s, when the hard and fast rules of the Victorian age were discarded, and everyone is now free to experiment to their heart's content. The art schools have worked hard in this direction, and the study of art and embroidery has been encouraged in the day schools, where much good work has been produced by young people. Invariably, however, there are still those among the adult population, who, when seeking to take up the craft of canvas embroidery, maintain that they are unwilling or unable to produce their own designs, and who readily resort to the ever-available canvas-work kits, the designs of which, one must admit, have improved considerably over the years and have in some cases been brought up to a level, which is more suitable for a modern piece of embroidery. The ideal way of working must, however, still be for the indivi-

The Nativity, worked by Rose Cussens, 1966   A canvas-work panel in tent stitch, worked with silk and vegetable-dyed wools. The whole design is outlined in white silk. It was based on a Christmas card and adapted to canvas work

dual person to create and develop his or her own design.

Short courses on canvas work are held in this country from time to time, some at the Royal School of Needlework and others at the Embroiderers' Guild, both at their headquarters in Hampton Court and at their numerous branches all over the country. In the United States of America there is a very keen interest in the subject, and workshops dealing with it are often held in many parts of that vast country, particularly in association with the Embroiderers' Guild of America. Whether canvas embroidery is, however, to experience a period of real progress in the future, or whether it will decline, is something which will depend very much upon the ability of the embroidery teachers, both in this country and elsewhere in the world, to encourage their students to create their own good designs for this work and to reproduce them in exciting ways upon the canvas.

Designing for canvas work

Clock Face, designed and worked by Thelma King, 1981
Four panels are shown, which contain images of birds.
They are worked in many different stitches, including
tent, French, Smyrna, Cretan and Hungarian on a background of long-legged cross stitch

Obtaining a suitable design for a piece of canvas
work is by no means an impossible task for a
beginner to undertake. Design is simply the art of
placing shapes and lines together within a given
area, so that they form a pleasant and well-balanced
whole. It is important to see that, when an arrange-

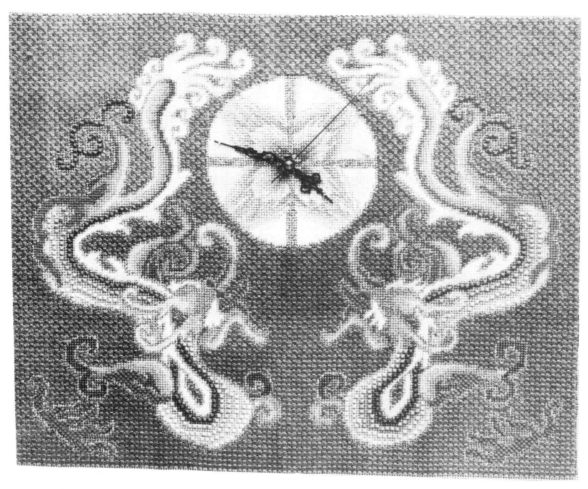

Clock Face, designed and worked by Thelma King, 1981. This piece has a Chinese-style design. It is worked on 16-mesh canvas in tent, Smyrna and back stitches. The background stitch is wheatsheaf half-drop with back stitch

ment of shapes is worked out for a design, the background areas left between these shapes are themselves attractive and well-balanced. Beginners often have the habit of leaving background areas in a design, which are much too large in comparison with the main areas of design.

When starting to prepare a design for use in canvas work, it is also necessary to have clearly in mind the purpose for which the finished work is intended, whether it is to serve some practical purpose as a cover for a cushion, a chair seat or a stool top, or whether it is to be put to a purely decorative use as a wall-hanging or picture, a mirror surround, or a cover for a lamp base or a clock face. If a practical use is decided upon, the nature of the design will be limited by the fact that it will need to be worked with materials that are both strong and durable and in stitches which will stand up to prolonged wear. A design for a purely decorative piece of canvas work will not be

limited in this way at all. Many different types of material may be used in the working of such pieces; the canvas need not be fully covered with stitchery and may have an irregular shape; and objects of various kinds, such as jewels, beads and shells, may be incorporated into the design, together with metal threads, decorative leather and coloured glass. The last of these materials, coloured glass, has been used to place behind the canvas, when areas have been cut out, and it has resulted in very pleasant decorative effects.

In preparing designs for use in working various types of furniture coverings, the nature of the stitches, which will be used, must be continually

167

borne in mind. If tent stitch, which is one of the strongest canvas-work stitches for this purpose, is chosen for the working, the design must be one which contains plenty of detail and avoids large areas of one flat colour, as tent stitch is a linear stitch, excellent for working curves, as well as straight lines, and also for shading, but quite unsuitable for working large areas of unbroken colour. When large areas of background have to be worked in tent stitch, the result is greatly improved if several shades of a colour are used. The use of square stitches, such as rice stitch, in conjunction with tent stitch for the working of furniture coverings permits designs to be employed which have larger areas of one colour than could be satisfactorily worked in tent stitch alone. The textural effect of the square stitch will give the necessary character to such large areas of colour. Where,

Geometric count-stitch patterns

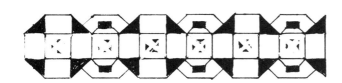

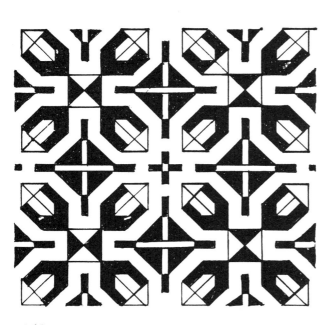

however, a design has many curved lines, a certain difficulty is presented to a worker using square stitches, who may be unable to avoid some distortion of the original line of the design, which will give it a clumsy and formless appearance. This danger can, however, be overcome by first using tent stitch to outline the curved shape of the design and by filling in small areas left between blocks of square stitches and the curved outlines with partly-worked square stitches or cross stitches and, where only single threads of canvas have to be covered, with tent stitch. (In America this process is called the use of 'compensation stitches').

When it comes to the actual preparation of a design for use in canvas embroidery, one may choose between the all-over count-stitch pattern, which is very useful for the working of furniture coverings, and the completely free type of pictorial or abstract design, suitable for wall panels and hangings. No really elaborate design is needed for working a count-stitch pattern, and a simple chart is often used as a guide by the worker, the only skill then needed being the ability to count the threads accurately.

Such patterns were used, as we have already seen, by Louisa Pesel, when she prepared designs for the production of kneelers for Winchester Cathedral during the 1930s. She took certain patterns from seventeenth century samplers, on which they had been worked in back stitch, and developed them for use on canvas by filling in the design with different stitches, such as cross stitch, long-legged cross stitch and tent stitch.

For the embroiderer who wishes to do something freer and more creative than the working of count-stitch patterns, good designs already traced upon canvas are available. Here I am thinking of prepared canvases, which are the work of professional designers, and not the coloured and trammed canvases sold in many needlework shops, which are only poor imitations of embroideries of former days or attempts to produce in embroidery copies of certain well-known paintings. Eventually, however, those embroiderers, who want to be truly creative and produce a completely original piece of canvas work, should attempt to make a design for themselves.

Sources of design

Nature has always provided the chief source of ideas for designs, and anyone with a good sense of design can find numerous pleasing shapes in plants and flowers, which will yield good ideas for designs in canvas work. Even more mundane and every-day objects can also be used in this way by those who have the ability to observe clearly the design potential in what is revealed to them. A useful way for a beginner to proceed is to take photographs of various natural objects, and from enlarged prints, taken from such photographs, it is often possible to select some interesting details, which will serve as inspiration for designs. Yet another method of proceeding, which appeals to some beginners, is to use a 'finder' for selecting an interesting element in a picture — either one taken by themselves, or even a picture in a magazine. Such a 'finder' is a piece of card with a rectangular or circular aperture cut out of it. It is placed upon a chosen picture, so that it isolates a small, interesting section of the latter, which can then be drawn up, enlarged and developed to give a suitable design.

For the person, who finds all of these methods of obtaining a design too difficult to use, one good way of proceeding is to cut shapes in paper and move them around within the outline shape required until a pleasing arrangement is found. Tissue paper is ideal for this purpose, as the shapes can be overlapped and will thus suggest degrees of tone, which can be very helpful when the final colour scheme is worked out. When a satisfactory arrangement of shapes has been arrived at, a sheet of tracing-paper should be placed over the whole design and the outline of the shapes should be traced on to it. If the paper shapes have been arranged upon the actual piece of canvas, which is going to be worked, then the outline should be drawn directly on to the canvas itself by means of a brush and Indian ink, or with a water-proof fibre-tipped pen. It must be a *waterproof* pen, if one is used, so that, if there is any need to stretch (block) the piece when it is finished, there will be no danger of staining the work, should it have to be dampened. A design obtained in this way will provide the basis upon which further connecting lines may be superimposed to give unity to the whole design.

Another source of designs for embroidery, and one which should not be despised, is doodling. If a number of doodles are drawn on a sheet of paper, the one which finally appeals as the most attractive can then be enlarged to the size required for a piece of canvas work, and additional lines can be drawn in to break up any areas which appear to lack sufficient interest. In doing this it is important to bear in mind the decorative value of background space and to give such areas as much attention and additional embellishment as the

Five worked canvas panels, based on Anchor stencilled designs, which are produced by J & P Coats of Glasgow. These are worked on single-mesh canvas of 18 threads to the inch, using tapisserie wools and stranded cotton. The designs of these attractive, modern, commercial canvases show a great improvement on those produced a few years ago. Even today, however, it is still possible to obtain in some needlework shops replicas of such Victorian designs as that of the *Last Supper*, which was based on Leonardo da Vinci's famous painting. 1 *Dreamland* 2 *Blue Trees* 3 *Brown Scape* 4 *Rural Setting* 5 *Pink Clouds*

main areas of the design. Doodles using string are particularly useful for creating geometric designs for use in canvss work.

Cross sections of seed-pods, vegetables and fruit can provide yet another source of ideas for designs, particularly if they are examined under a powerful magnifying glass, or if thin sections from them are placed between glass and projected on to a screen, from which they can be photographed.

Further ideas for designs can be readily found among the many objects we observe around us in the world: the interesting shapes of machinery and industrial equipment, such as pylons, scaffolding and collections of materials stacked in timber yards, can all provide a fruitful source of ideas for both geometric and free designs. Photographs from industrial and scientific magazines and newspapers will often supply exciting shapes, which can be developed into workable designs for embroidery.

Shadows of various objects or reflections from them are often projected on to a wall or the ground, or upon a table or the floor or ceiling in a room, and these can be lively and quite exciting sources of design, as can also the branches of a tree silhouetted against the sky.

Found objects can often form actual parts of a design by being attached to the canvas and having a suitable design in stitchery built up around them. Such things as interestingly shaped pieces of stone or shells collected on a beach make excellent objects for use in this way, as do also beads and jewels or even old coins.

Enlarging a design

Sometimes it is necessary to enlarge a design in order to be able to fill a particular area of canvas which has to be worked. To do this the original drawing is enclosed within a square or rectangle, which is then divided up by drawing a grid of squares upon it, or a tracing can be made of the original design and the grid of squares can be drawn upon that. A larger rectangle of the size

Mississippi This shows a worked Anchor Tapestry charted design. The size is $16\frac{1}{8}$ in. x $9\frac{1}{2}$ in. (41 cm x 24 cm) *J & P Coats (UK), Glasgow*

Finder in Use to select shapes for a design from a photograph of a collection of twigs

Finder made from two right-angle pieces of card, which can be moved up and down to make a larger or smaller aperture

required for the piece of work should also be drawn up on a sheet of paper and should be divided up in a similar way by means of a grid of larger squares. If it is wished to double the size of the original design, this can easily be achieved by covering it with a grid of, let us say, half-inch (12.5 mm) squares, whilst the enlarged drawing will be made on a grid of one-inch (25 mm) squares. The grids on both the original small drawing and the enlargement should be numbered from the bottom left-hand corner both vertically and horizontally, and the enlarged drawing can then be made by carefully matching the position of each line on the new drawing with its position on the original design as shown by the grid.

If an enlargement has to be made to a size which cannot be calculated readily as a multiple of the original dimensions of a design, it can be done by adopting the following method. A rectangle (ABCD in the illustration), which is the same size and shape as the one enclosing the original design, is first drawn on paper and its base AB is extended to the point E to give the length required in the enlargement. A perpendicular line is erected at point E, and the diagonal AC of the original rectangle is extended until it cuts this perpendicular line at point F. The side AD of the smaller rectangle is then extended to the same length as EF, and the new larger rectangle AEFG is completed. In this method of working the two rectangles can be best divided into the necessary grids by folding them into halves, quarters and possibly eights. (See illustration).

A Reflection from a wine-glass

174

Colour

Colour is a very important adjunct to design, as it can be the means of helping the designer to create atmosphere: some colours suggest a pleasant sensation of light and warmth, whilst others reflect sadness and despair by seeming dark and cold. The so-called warm colours, red, orange and yellow, which are related in Nature to sunlight and fire, are also the colours which in an artistic creation can suggest vigour and excitement, whilst the blues and greens, the so-called cool colours, which are associated with the sky, the sea and natural vegetation, suggest calm and rest.

There are many theories of colour harmony which can be studied and from which helpful suggestions may be obtained, but it has to be realised that there are no absolute rules which can be generally applied to the use of colour in doing embroidery. The individual embroiderer must in the end decide what effect he or she wishes to achieve, and probably the best advice to follow in

Method of enlarging a design A The original small sketch enclosed within a grid of one- inch (25 mm) squares
B Sketch 'A' enlarged to double its size within a grid of two-inch squares (50 mm)
C A method of enlarging which introduces some distortion of the original design. Here it is vertical distortion

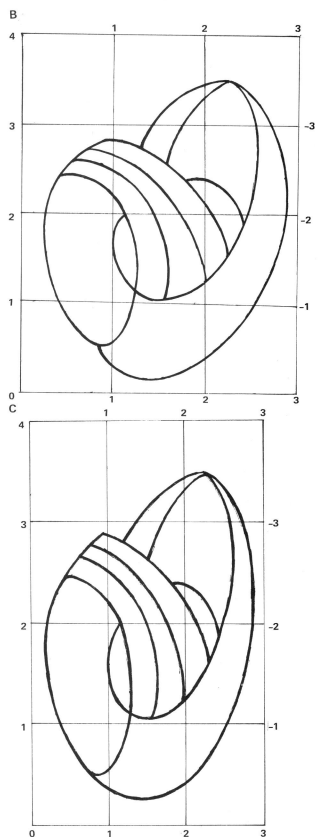

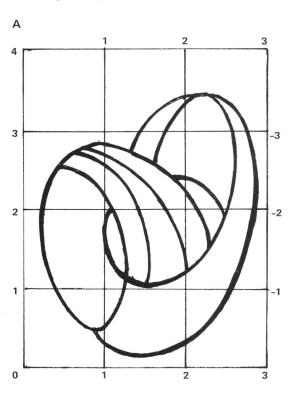

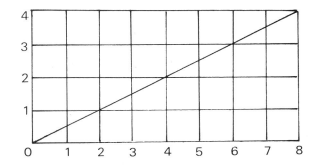

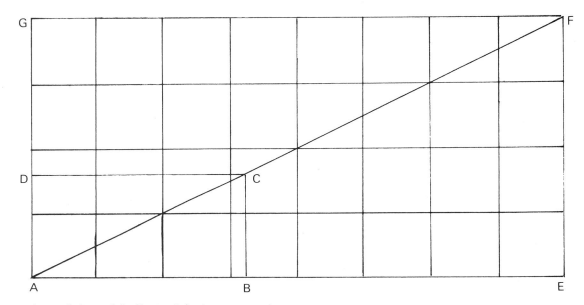

The method of enlarging a drawing to a certain fixed length and width

order to bring originality and freshness to a piece of work is to observe and draw inspiration from the wealth of colour seen in Nature. One thing that is there revealed is that the real quality of a colour varies according to what other colours are placed beside it: if a strong green is, for instance, placed beside a neutral grey, the grey will appear reddish, and if a strong red is placed beside it, the grey will acquire a greenish tinge; a pale yellow, when placed beside red, will cause the red to appear richer in colour, and purple will cause it to seem paler. If it is thought necessary to retain as far as possible the characteristic effect of certain colours, they can be isolated from proximity to other colours by surrounding them with a small area of black or white, but even the neutralising effect of these colours cannot prevent a slight change of tone in the colours they enclose, black causing the other colour to seem lighter in tone, and white causing it to appear darker. It will also be noticed

that an area of colour, when surrounded by black, will appear larger, than a similar area of the same colour surrounded by white.

The relative intensity or brightness of colours, which can be observed in Nature to derive from whether an object is near to or remote from the observer, can also be seen to apply to embroidery, where areas worked in bright colours will always seem to be nearer to the viewer than those worked in dull colours, and this fact should be borne in mind when building up a colour scheme for a piece of canvas work. Even when a picture or wall

Seascape, designed and worked by June Haysom, 1976 ▷
This panel shows interesting texture, which has been achieved by the use of a wide variety of canvas-work stitches

Detail of a panel, which shows the textural quality that can be achieved, when the bulky Rhodes stitch is worked in conjunction with the much flatter cross-cornered cushion stitch

The Old Church, Shanklin, Isle of Wight, worked by Nellie J Old, 1982   A further example of fine textural effects, achieved by the use of a variety of stitches

178

A fine textural effect is created in this detail from a larger
panel of canvas work, in which long stitches, worked in
coton perlé, contrast well with the sumptuous confusion
of Rhodes, Smyrna, cross and tent stitches

179

An attractive textural effect has been created here by working many different stitches with raffene and wool

hanging is in the process of being worked, the embroiderer is advised to prop it up against the wall from time to time to allow it to be viewed from a distance, as it will be when it is completed. This will sometimes show the worker that a change in the chosen colour scheme is required, as the effect of the colours already used, when seen from a distance, may be quite different from what it seemed at close quarters during the actual working. It should also be remembered, when choosing colours to use in a piece of canvas embroidery, that the yarn appears brighter when seen in the skein, than it does when worked on canvas, and, if a wall panel is being worked, the colours need to be reasonably bright in order to resist the fading which will eventually occur over the years.

Texture

As we have already noticed, tonal variations, caused by the juxtaposition of certain colours, occur in the development of suitable colour schemes for working canvas embroidery and play an important part in the final result. Similarly textural variations, which are occasioned by the use of the wide range of different canvas-work stitches, also bring about changes of tone in the colours used and give to the work its true character. It is an excellent idea to limit the number of colours used in working a design, and to try to get the maximum effect from them by employing a variety of stitches to give both interesting texture and changes of tone. By using both large and small stitches in working an area of one colour, it is possible to produce shadows, which in their turn can introduce considerable tonal variation. The embroiderer should, however, choose carefully the particular stitch, which is best suited to each section of a design, and should try not to develop a preference for one stitch to the exclusion of others. There are now so many stitches to choose from, that it should not prove too difficult to discover just the right one for every occasion, and thus avoid indiscriminate use of stitches just for the sake of using them. The best results in canvas work are achieved, when the finished design preserves the special attributes of this old craft, and is worked in such a way, that what is finally produced really looks like a piece of embroidery and not under any circumstances like a painting.

Stitchery

Stitches and stitch patterns

As we have already seen in considering the history of canvas work, the main stitch used up to the seventeenth century, and probably the oldest one that was employed in doing this work, was tent stitch. This was followed closely by cross stitch and plaited stitch, and a few years later by long-legged cross, eyelet and rococo stitches. John Taylor, the self-styled 'water poet', in his book, *The Needles Excellency*, published in 1640, gives a list of stitches then in use, which specifically includes 'tent worke', cross stitch and back stitch, and several others, the names of which are unrecognisable to us in the twentieth century. Irish stitch is one stitch mentioned, and it is thought by some people to be another name for Florentine stitch. This is quite possible, as what we generally call Florentine stitch in this country today became extremely popular all over the embroiderers' world, because it was an easy stitch to work and covered the background material quickly, but, as a result of its widespread use, it became burdened with many different names, such as flame stitch, long and short stitch, straight stitch, cushion stitch, and, in America, Hungarian or Bargello stitch. The most descriptive name is, of course, straight stitch, because that is what it actually is: all the individual stitches are vertical straight stitches, which are generally worked over four threads of the canvas, and they are used to build up stitch patterns. A much more attractive way of working with vertical straight stitches is what is called *point d'hongrie*, in which a pattern is built up with stitches of varying length.

The designs used in the early days of canvas work were of a kind which required to be worked in tent stitch in order to be able to produce the frequent changes in shades of a colour, which were needed for rendering the fine detail of a design. Today, however, when the modern type of design is generally worked on a much coarser kind of canvas, greater freedom is allowed to the worker, and a broader repertory of stitches is employed, than would formerly have been required.

Point d'hongrie or *Hungarian Variation*

Back view of tent stitch

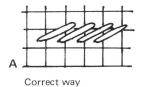

A

Correct way

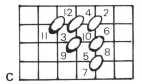

Diagonal Tent Stitch
(also known as Basket Weave)

C

B

Wrong way

Working from the top
downwards

Working from the
bottom upwards

Working from left to
right

Working from right to
left

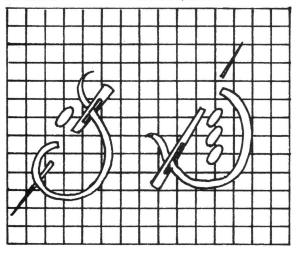

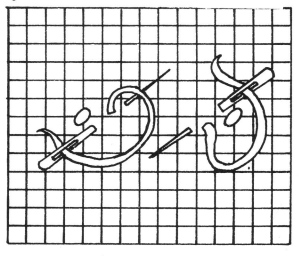

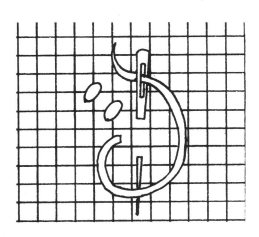

Working tent stitch diagonally downwards from the top left

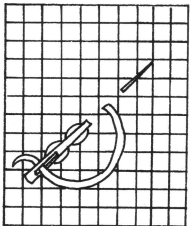

Working tent stitch diagonally
upwards from the bottom left-hand

Tent stitch (petit point)

Tent stitch is still the most important of all canvas-work stitches. Apart from back stitch, it is the smallest stitch which it is possible to use on canvas, and it is ideal for outlining parts of a design, for doing intricate shading and for use as a compensation stitch in certain small areas. A strong foundation material, such as canvas, when reinforced with tent stitch, which is taken into every hole in the mesh, makes one of the most durable fabrics and is highly suitable for furniture coverings. It should be stressed, however, that it is not an ideal stitch to use for working wide areas of plain ground in one colour, whether in the design or in the background, as it will create a very flat effect, if shading is not used.

There are two ways in which tent stitch is often worked, but only one of these is the correct method for use on canvas. Diagram (A) shows this method of working, and it also shows how the reverse side of the work should look. Diagram (B) shows the method of working the stitch, which is the wrong method for canvas work, although it is the correct way of working it on table linen. The reason why this second method is not the best for canvas work is revealed when the reverse side of the work is examined, where it is seen that only tiny vertical straight stitches appear, which leave many of the canvas threads uncovered.

A piece of canvas embroidery produced by this second method of working will not possess the same hard-wearing qualities which the correct method of working, with its long stitch on the reverse side, gives to the finished work, and it will appear somewhat thin and moth-eaten on the front.

Many magazines and books published on this subject state that, when working tent stitch, the best way to proceed is to work always from right to left, fastening off at the end of each row and starting again from the right. Otherwise, they say, a ridged effect will emerge. This is, of course, nonsense, as the detailed diagram (C) shows that the position of the needle has to be altered in order to continue working tent stitch in the reverse direction, and it is only when this information is ignored and the stitch is incorrectly worked from left to right, producing a small upright straight stitch on the reverse side instead of the normal long stitch, that a ridged effect will occur.

Another popular way of working tent stitch today is to work it diagonally across the canvas, a method of working generally known as basket weave. This method can only be used, however, for working a flat tent-stitch background and is no good for working tent stitch, when it is being used for shading purposes. It was a method of working which was introduced into Victorian England from France at some time in the last quarter of the nineteenth century, and it was adopted then in order to avoid the distortion of the canvas, which the old traditional method invariably caused, and to do away with the need for stretching (blocking) the work when it was finished.

Tent stitch (Petit point)

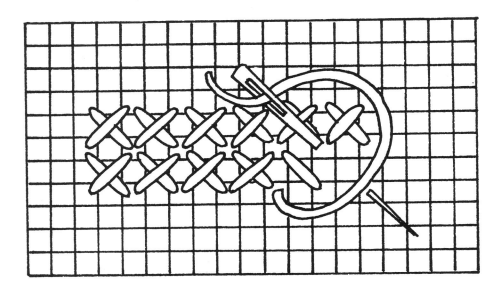

Cross stitch

This was often worked in the early days over one intersection of the canvas, but today it is generally worked over two intersections. It consists of two diagonal straight stitches, which cross one another at right-angles. The upper stitch of each cross must always be made in the same direction, and it is normal practice for it to be worked from bottom left to top right in each cross stitch. Better tension will be achieved in the working, if each individual cross stitch is completed before the next one is started.

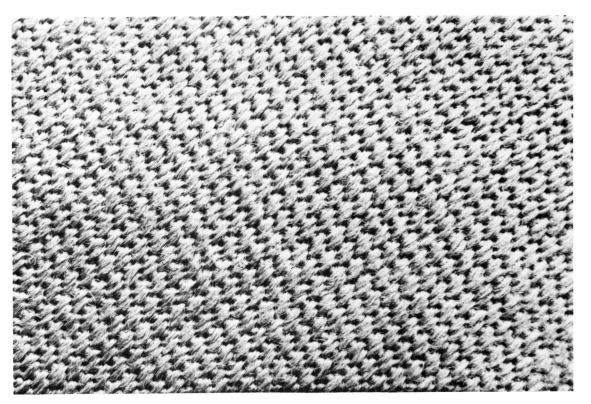

Cashmere stitch

This is a useful stitch for covering large areas of background and consists of a series of groups of three diagonal stitches. When worked from left to right, all three stitches in each group start immediately beneath one another, one over one intersection of the canvas and two over two intersections. As it is usual to start this stitch at the top left-hand corner of the area to be covered, and to work diagonally downwards, each unit of three stitches will commence one thread of the canvas to the right of the point where the last stitch in the previous unit began.

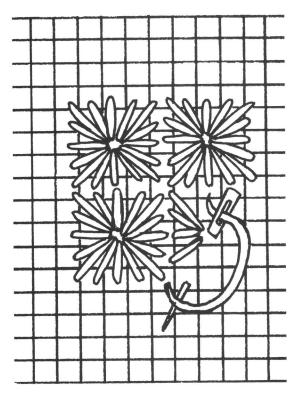

Eyelet stitch

This stitch is usually worked over a square of four threads of the canvas. From each of the holes around the sides of the square a stitch is taken over two threads of the canvas and down into the centre hole. Care must be taken, when working an eyelet, to arrange that the last stitch to enter the centre hole is put in the correct position for pulling the yarn away from the hole, when it is being taken to the point for starting work on the next eyelet. It is essential to do this, in order to keep the centre hole open and uncluttered.

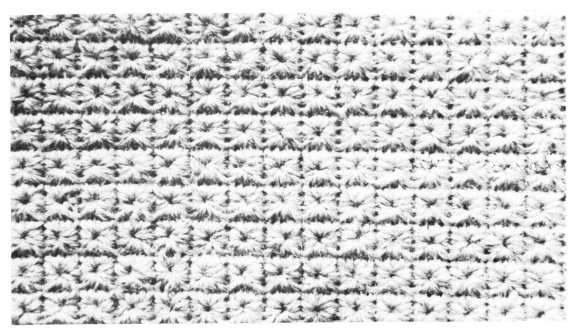

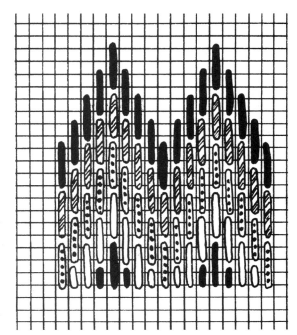

Florentine stitch

A very popular stitch, which consists of a series of vertical straight stitches, worked over four horizontal threads of the canvas, each individual stitch rising or falling by two threads above or below the previous one. The best known, and most popular way of working, produces a zigzag or flame pattern, the effect of which is accentuated by a skilful use of colour.

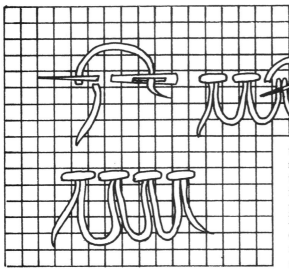

Ghiordes knot (Turkey rug knot)

This stitch is started from the front of the canvas and is worked from the bottom left-hand corner of the area to be covered. The loose end of the yarn is held between forefinger and thumb of the left hand, whilst the needle is taken under one vertical thread of the canvas, moving from right to left. Then, with the working yarn held loosely, the needle should be put under the next vertical thread of the canvas to the right and, moving once more from right to left, it should be brought up through the same hole in the canvas where the first stitch was started, and in such a way that it passes under the loop of the working yarn. This loop should then be tightened by pulling the two ends of the yarn down firmly. The process is repeated under the next vertical thread of the canvas to the right, whilst a loop of the yarn is at the same time held down by the thumb, and it is continued thus, until a whole row of stitches has been completed. The working yarn should be cut at the end of the row, and the next row of stitches should be begun on the left-hand side, two threads of the canvas above and one thread to the right of the first stitch in the first row, so that the rows of stitches will be staggered. Finally, the loops of yarn can be cut and trimmed to form a pile with an approximate depth of ¼ in. (6 mm).

Gobelin stitch

The name Gobelin covers a whole group of straight satin stitches. The basic form of this stitch, which is also known as Gros Point, should be worked in horizontal rows from top to bottom of the area to be covered, the first row being worked from right to left, the second from left to right, and so on. Start by taking a diagonal stitch upwards over two horizontal threads of the canvas and one vertical thread to the right. The next stitch is then begun two horizontal threads of the canvas down from this point and two vertical threads to the left and is worked in the same way as the first stitch. This process is repeated until a complete row of stitches has been worked across the canvas. The second row then begins with the needle being brought up through the canvas at the point where the last stitch but one in the first row had begun, and being taken down over two horizontal threads of the canvas and one vertical thread to the left. For the next stitch in this row the needle is brought up

two horizontal threads of the canvas above this point and two vertical threads to the right, and the process is repeated until the second row has been worked. The diagram shows this method of working, which is thought to be the best for getting the maximum amount of wool on the reverse side of the canvas, and thus giving the finished embroidery a fuller and better appearance.

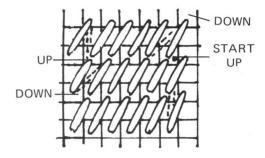

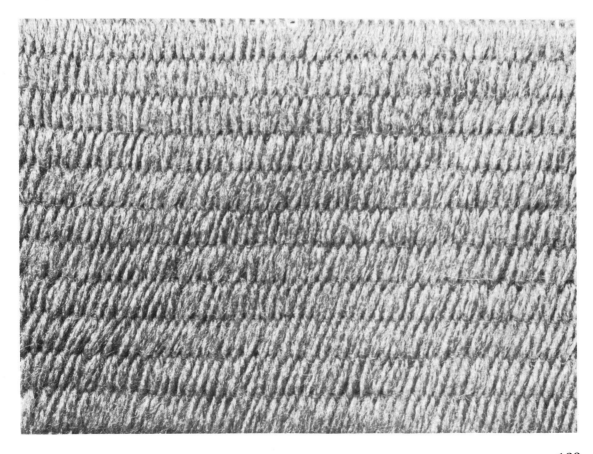

189

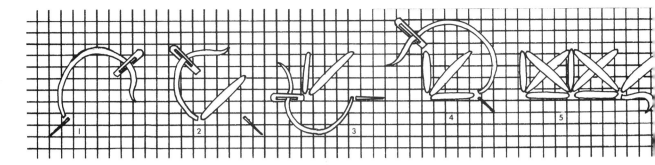

Italian two-sided stitch

This stitch consists of four individual stitches, three of which radiate from the bottom left-hand corner of a square, which extends over four threads of the canvas, and one stitch, which is taken from the bottom right-hand corner of the square to the top left-hand corner, thus passing over the other diagonal and forming a cross stitch within a square of straight stitches, when all the adjoining stitches have been worked. The yarn is brought out at the bottom right-hand corner of the square, when one group of four stitches has been completed, ready to begin the next group.

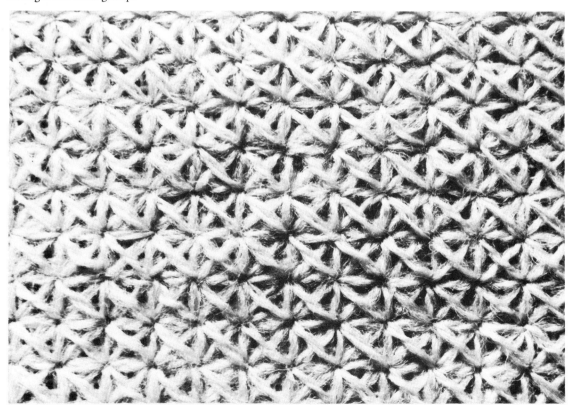

190

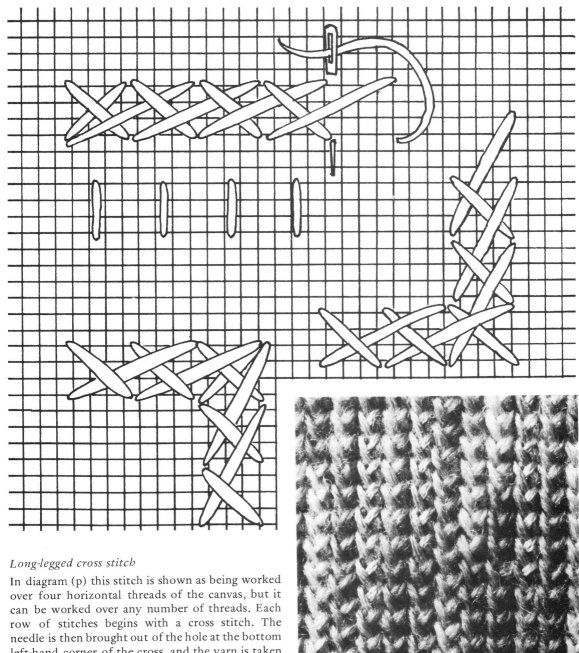

Long-legged cross stitch

In diagram (p) this stitch is shown as being worked over four horizontal threads of the canvas, but it can be worked over any number of threads. Each row of stitches begins with a cross stitch. The needle is then brought out of the hole at the bottom left-hand corner of the cross, and the yarn is taken up obliquely over four horizontal and eight vertical threads of the canvas to the right. It is brought out again four horizontal threads of the canvas immediately below this point, and an oblique stitch is put in, going up to the left over four horizontal and four vertical threads of the canvas. The process is continued by bringing out the needle four horizontal threads immediately below and repeating the sequence, but without the initial cross stitch.

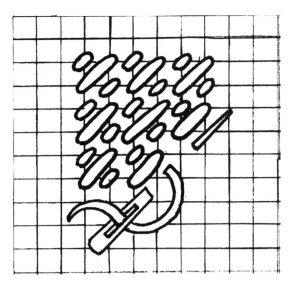

Mosaic stitch

This neat and attractive square stitch has the effect, when worked, of a small cross stitch. It is useful for backgrounds, and can be successfully employed for shading. Each stitch consists of a group of three diagonal stitches and covers a square of two horizontal and two vertical threads of the canvas, the first individual stitch being over one intersection of the canvas, the second over two intersections, and the third over one. It is, in fact, two tent stitches with one stitch, taken over two intersections of the canvas, placed in between them.

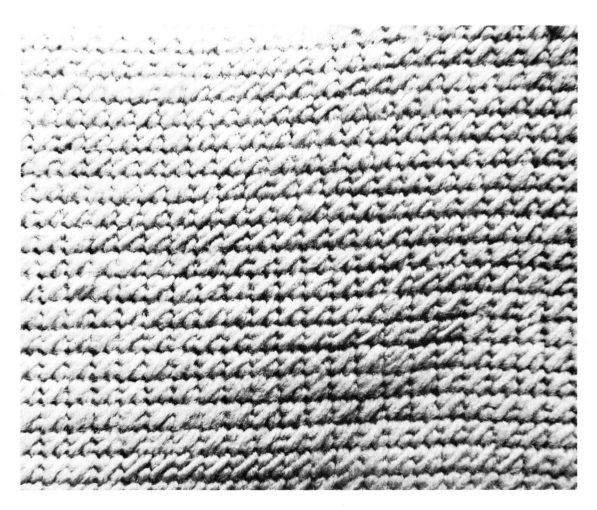

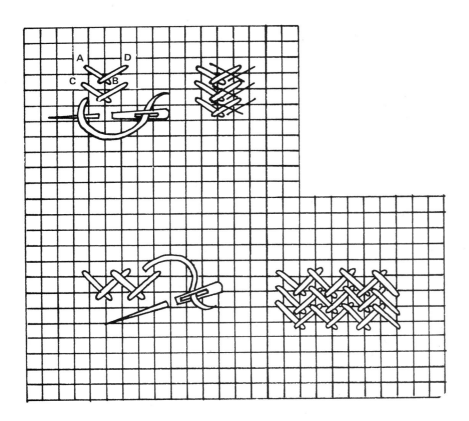

Plaited stitch

This stitch can be worked either horizontally or vertically across the canvas. In the diagram, which shows it worked horizontally, the needle is first brought up at point A, and the yarn is taken down to the right over two horizontal and two vertical threads of the canvas to point B. The needle is then taken back to the left under one thread of the canvas to point C, and the yarn is taken up over two horizonatal and two vertical threads of the canvas to the right to point D. By once again taking the needle back to the left under one thread of the canvas, it is ready to begin the second stitch in the row. Subsequent rows of Plaited Stitch are worked by starting at a point one horizontal thread of the canvas below the first stitch in the row above.

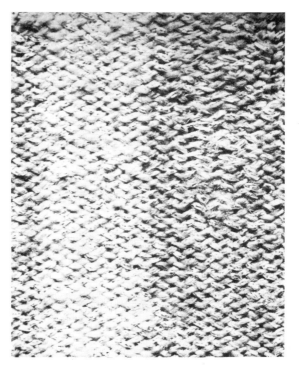

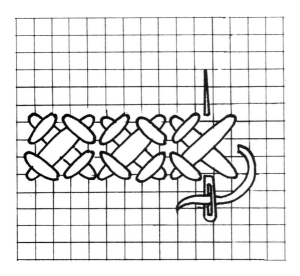

Rice stitch (Also known as Crossed Corners)

This stitch is formed by working a cross stitch over four threads of the canvas, and then putting in over each leg of the cross a diagonal back stitch, which is worked over two intersections of the canvas, as shown in the diagram.

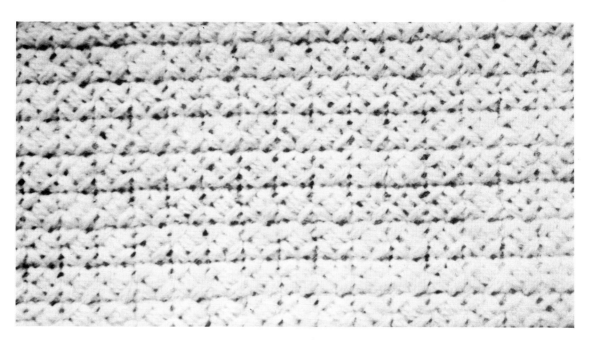

194

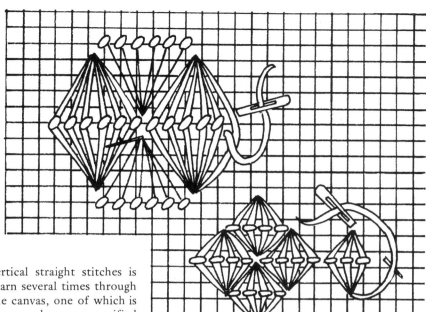

Rococo stitch

An even number of vertical straight stitches is worked by passing the yarn several times through the same two holes in the canvas, one of which is directly above the other and an unspecified number of threads of the canvas distant from it. The individual stitches are spread out and each one is tied down to a thread of the canvas, so as to produce a balanced effect. If the stitches pass over an even number of horizontal threads of the canvas, a back stitch should be used to tie them down, but, if they pass over an uneven number of canvas threads, a tent stitch must be used to fix them, as shown in the diagram.

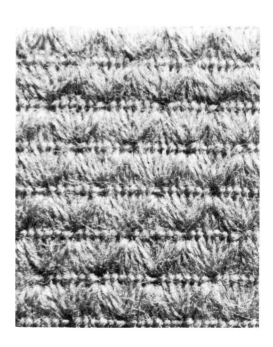

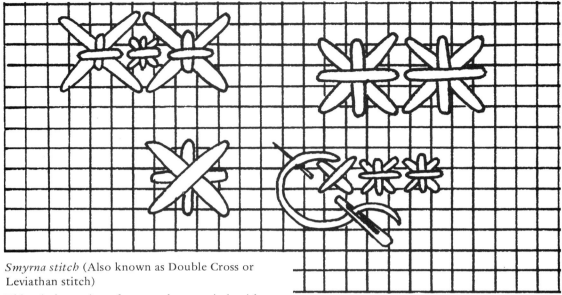

Smyrna stitch (Also known as Double Cross or Leviathan stitch)

This stitch consists of a normal cross stitch with an upright cross stitch worked over it. It can be worked over two, four or more even numbers of threads of the canvas. The top stitches of the upright cross stitches should all be worked in one direction, either all horizontally or all vertically.

All the stitches given above have been in common use for many years, but the following are new stitches, which have been evolved during the last twenty years or more.

Broad Cross stitch

This very attractive stitch occupies a square of six threads of the canvas. Three vertical straight stitches are worked first, and then the three horizontal stitches are put in across them by bringing the needle up for the first horizontal stitch at a point two horizontal threads of the canvas down and two vertical threads to the left of the point where the first vertical stitch began, and taking the yarn across the three vertical stitches to a similar point on the other side. The other two horizontal stitches are then worked immediately beneath the first. A row of such stitches is worked horizontally across the canvas, as shown in the diagram. To work the second row of Broad Crosses the easiest method of proceeding is to begin with the centre stitch of the three vertical stitches: this is done by bringing the needle up six horizontal threads of the canvas immediately below the hole where the third horizontal stitches in the first and second Broad Crosses of the first row meet, and then taking the yarn down into this same hole. Another vertical stitch is put in on either side of this middle one, and the whole Broad Cross is completed as in the diagram.

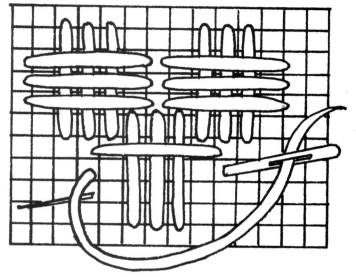

Broad Cross — diagonal

When Broad Cross is worked diagonally, it takes the same form as when it is worked horizontally, but individual stitches follow the line of the true diagonal of the canvas and are taken over five intersections of the canvas.

197

Compact Filling stitch

The best way to work this stitch is diagonally from top left to bottom right of the area to be covered. The yarn is brought up through the canvas three vertical threads to the right of the top left-hand corner of this area, and a vertical straight stitch is taken down over three horizontal threads of the canvas. The needle is then brought up three vertical threads to the left, and a horizontal stitch is taken back over these three threads and down into the same hole at the base of the first stitch. Two oblique stitches, each one over two intersections of the canvas, are then put in, one beside the other, in a position immediately beneath the right-angle formed by the first two stitches. (See diagram.

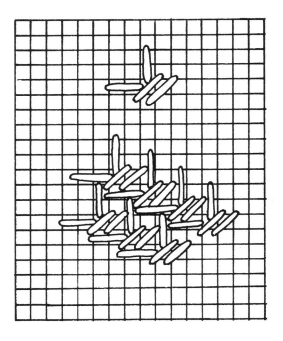

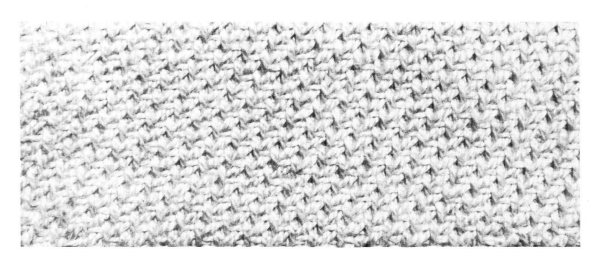

Cross Plus Two stitch

This is a very attractive stitch, which, when it is worked with a fine, tightly-spun wool, gives a lace-like appearance to the embroidery. A Cross stitch is worked over six horizontal and four vertical threads of the canvas. A vertical straight stitch over six horizontal threads of the canvas is then taken over the centre of the cross, and a horizontal straight stitch over four canvas threads is worked at the base of the cross. Vertical rows of this stitch are worked with a half-drop pattern, as shown in diagram.

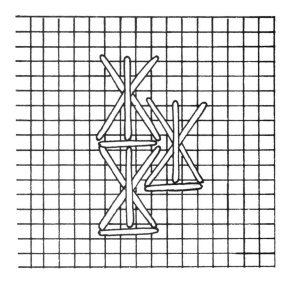

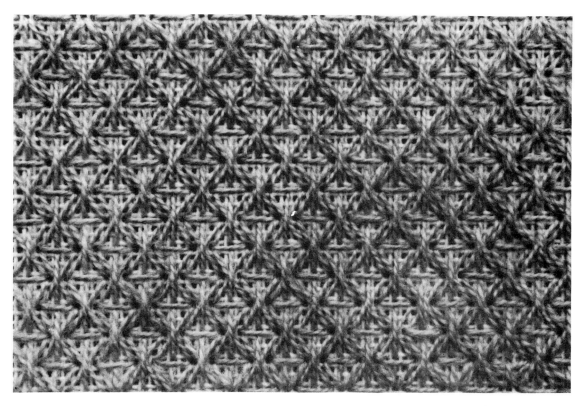

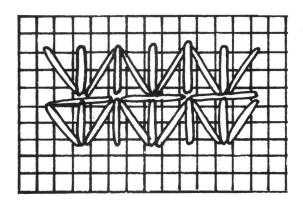

Crow's Foot stitch

Three individual straight stitches, all radiating from a central hole at the base of the crow's foot, are worked over three horizontal threads of the canvas. The centre stitch of the three is a vertical stitch over three horizontal threads, and those on either side of it are oblique stitches over three horizontal and two vertical threads of the canvas. A single vertical straight stitch, worked over three horizontal threads, separates these groups of stitches. A horizontal back stitch over four vertical threads of the canvas is placed between successive rows of stitches.

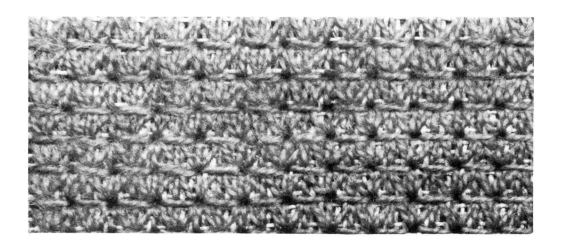

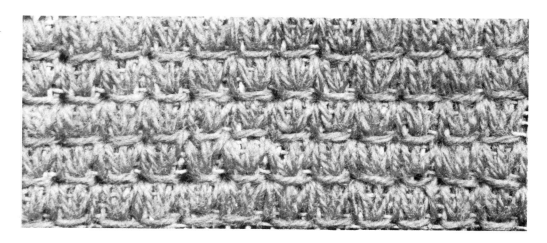

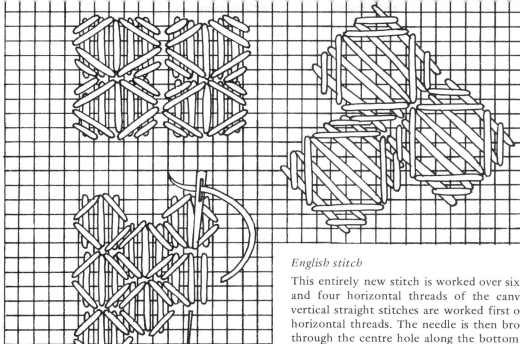

English stitch

This entirely new stitch is worked over six vertical and four horizontal threads of the canvas. Five vertical straight stitches are worked first over four horizontal threads. The needle is then brought up through the centre hole along the bottom edge of the stitch and is taken down into the centre hole on the left-hand side. It then emerges from the centre hole on the right-hand side, to be taken down again into the centre hole on the bottom edge. From this point the needle is then brought up through the centre hole on the top edge of the stitch and taken down into the centre hole on the left-hand side. It is brought up once again through the centre hole on the right-hand side and is taken down into the centre hole at the top. A small diagonal stitch over two intersections of the canvas is then worked over each corner of the group of vertical stitches, outside and parallel to the four longer diagonal stitches just worked.

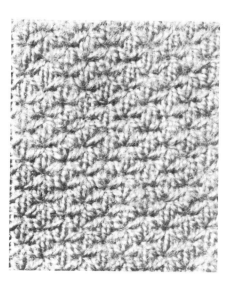

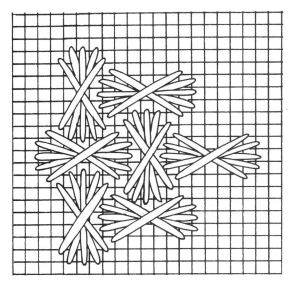

Fan Vaulting stitch

This stitch consists of five individual stitches forming a cross. Three of these stitches are over eight threads of the canvas and are worked first, the centre one of the three being a straight stitch, with the other two forming a cross, which lies over the first stitch. The remaining two stitches in the group are over six threads of the canvas, and they make a final cross over all the others. In working a complete row of Fan Vaulting stitches the crosses are placed alternately in a vertical or a horizontal position, so that they fit neatly together, as shown in the diagram.

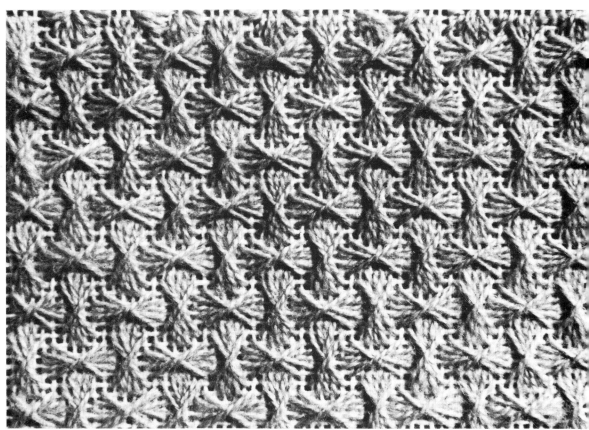

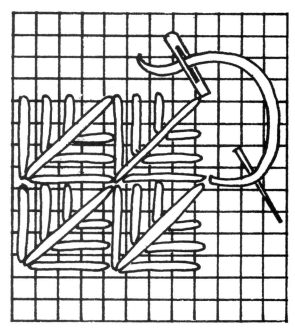

Four, Three, Two Cross stitch

This is a square stitch, worked over four threads of the canvas. First of all three vertical stitches over four, three and two horizontal threads of the canvas respectively are worked side by side, the first stitch forming the left-hand side of the square and the other two having their top ends on the top edge of the square, with their lower ends each rising one horizontal thread above the lower end of the stitch before. A group of three horizontal stitches of the same size is then put in at right-angles to the first group, so that a square of stitches is formed, and this is finished off when a diagonal stitch is taken from the bottom left-hand corner up to the top right.

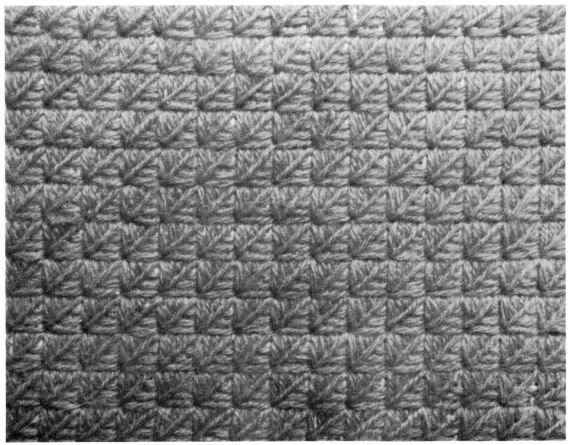

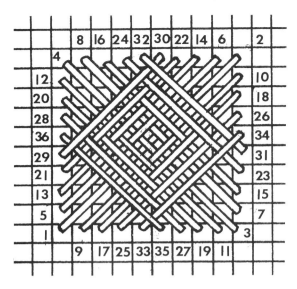

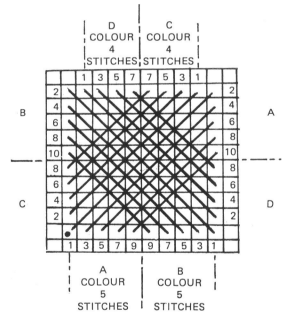

This stitch can be worked in various sizes, and the diagram shows how it appears when worked over a square with an uneven number of threads of the canvas. The individual stitches are numbered in order of working, and it will be noticed that the method of working follows a regular pattern, until the last stitch is put in, when the needle is slipped under instead of over stitch 29-30, the last stitch it passes before entering the canvas at hole 36.

204

Norwich stitch can also be worked over an even number of threads of the canvas, but in that case the appearance of the stitch will be slightly different, as the final four stitches will go into the same holes in the canvas at the centre of each side of the square, without crossing over one another.

An interesting effect can be achieved by using threads of more than one colour in the working of Norwich Stitch.

Another version of this stitch is shown in diagram (k). Here the order in which the individual stitches are worked gives the completed Norwich Stitch a solid area of yarn on the reverse side of the canvas, which means that pieces of embroidery in which it is employed will also acquire extra strength. This version of Norwich stitch can be worked in a single colour, or, if so desired, in a combination of four different colours of yarn. If the decision is made to use four different colours in the working, then four needles will be required for the purpose, which makes the stitch appear somewhat complicated, but, if the numbered diagram is followed carefully, all problems will disappear. The main trouble with using four needles in doing a piece of canvas work is the problem of where to park them, when they are not actually in use. Probably the best way to proceed is to have a roll of soft material pinned down on each side of the work, into which the needles can be placed to keep them out of the way while not being used. When several units have been worked in different colours, a very interesting tile-effect can be observed.

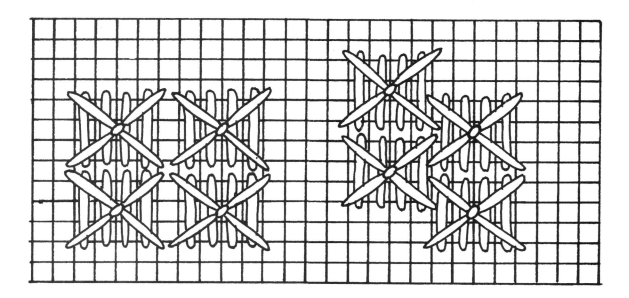

Pineapple stitch — Half-drop

When Pineapple stitch is worked diagonally across the canvas, the finished appearance, which it presents, is quite different from the way it appears, when it is worked in vertical or horizontal rows. Each group of stitches is dropped down two horizontal threads of the canvas lower than the group before it, and the stitches fit closer together, as shown in the diagram.

Pineapple stitch

Four vertical straight stitches over four horizontal threads of the canvas are worked first. A cross stitch, extending over four horizontal and five vertical threads of the canvas, is then put in over the top of these four straight stitches. This cross stitch is finally tied down in the centre by means of a small diagonal stitch over the central vertical thread of the canvas.

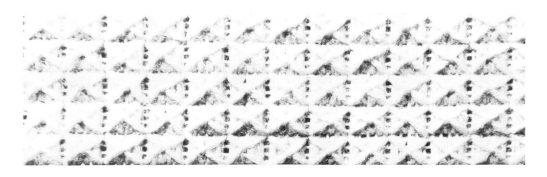

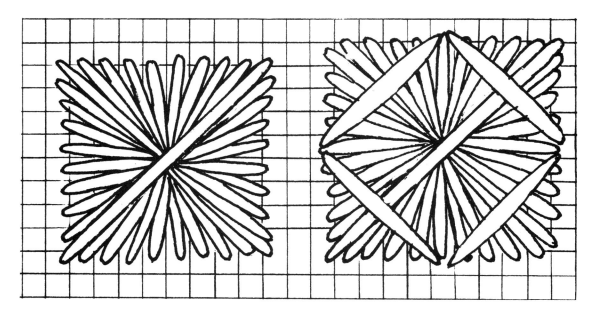

Rhodes stitch

This is a bulky square stitch, which may be worked over any number of threads of the canvas from a minimum of three horizontal and three vertical threads. The working consists of taking a stitch, which passes over the centre of the square, into every hole around the sides of the square, beginning with a stitch from the hole one vertical thread of the canvas to the right of the bottom left-hand corner, which is taken down into the hole one vertical thread to the left of the top right-hand corner of the square, and progressing right round the square, always proceeding in an anti-clockwise direction, to finish with a diagonal stitch from the top right-hand corner to the bottom left-hand corner of the square.

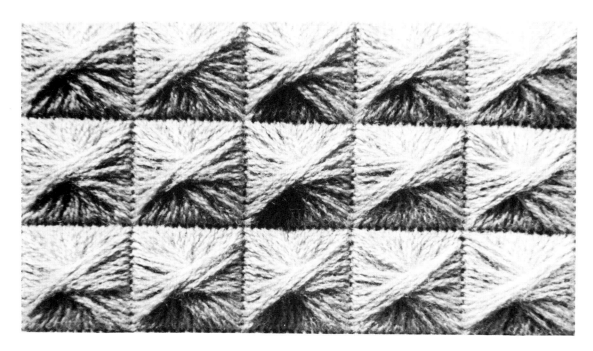

Half Rhodes stitch — half-drop

This stitch is worked in rows diagonally down across the area of canvas to be covered. It is, as the name implies, just half a normal Rhodes stitch, with the first individual stitch being taken diagonally from the bottom left-hand corner of the square to the top right-hand corner and the last stitch in each group from the bottom right-hand corner to the top left-hand corner. Each group of stitches after the first in each diagonal row is started half its depth below the previous group, and the diagram shows how this is done, when the stitch is worked over 6 threads of the canvas: the second group of stitches is begun by bringing up the needle 3 horizontal threads of the canvas below the bottom right-hand corner of the first group of stitches and 2 vertical threads to the left. In this way the second group of stitches is worked so that it fits closely beside the first group. This very attractive stitch can be worked over any even number of threads of the canvas.

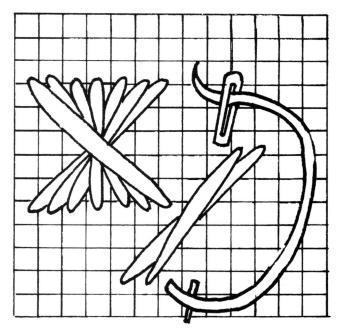

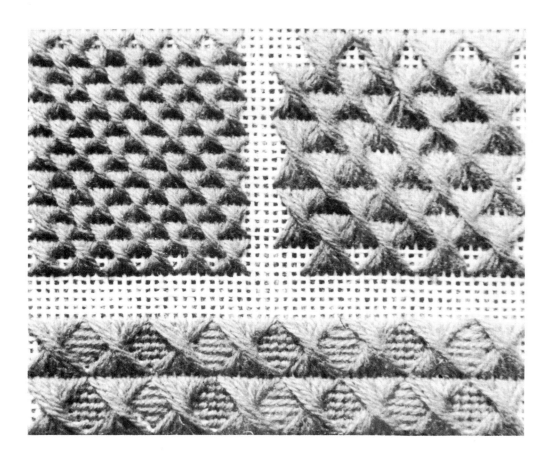

Materials and equipment

Canvas

Embroidery canvas is made from linen, hemp, cotton or gauze, the last-named being for use in making small, fine articles, such as evening bags. A plastic canvas, which has been used in the United States of America for the past few years, has also recently become available in this country. The two main types of canvas, which are suitable for canvas work, are the single thread (Congress) canvas, which is sometimes known as Mono, and the double-thread canvas, which is known as Penelope canvas. These canvases are available in a wide range of meshes, the mesh of a canvas being the number of threads to the inch, and they vary from as fine as 32 threads to the inch (25 mm) to as coarse as four double-threads to the inch (25 mm) in the type of canvas which is used for rug-making. The widths in which canvas is made also vary from 12 in. to 59 in. (30 cm to 150 cm), so it is necessary, when ordering a supply, to state the quantity, the width and the mesh required: eg one yard (or one metre) of 27 in. (69 cm) wide, 16 mesh single canvas, or, if Penelope, double canvas is preferred, one yard of 36 in. (91 cm) wide 16/32 mesh canvas.

For someone starting a piece of canvas work for the first time, the range of meshes available can be somewhat daunting, but a good rule to follow is that, if the design to be worked is a bold one without much detail, then a canvas with 12 or 14 threads to the inch (25 mm) would be the one to choose, and for a fairly fine and detailed design, a medium canvas with 16 or 18 threads to the inch (25 mm) would be a more suitable choice. A 14 or 16 mesh canvas is usually very good for working chair seats, church kneelers, stool tops, cushions, mirror surrounds and clock faces, as well as for pictures and small wall hangings, but, where very

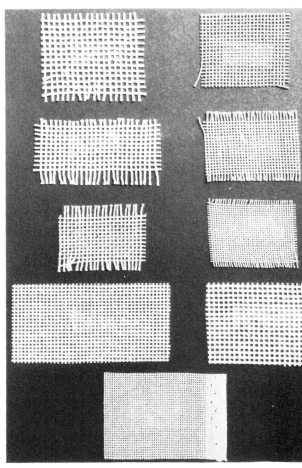

Single-mesh Cotton Canvases, which vary from 10-mesh to 24-mesh

The example shown at the bottom of the picture is a fine, coloured canvas of 24-mesh, which is dyed bright orange. The two examples above it are the recently-introduced interlocked canvas

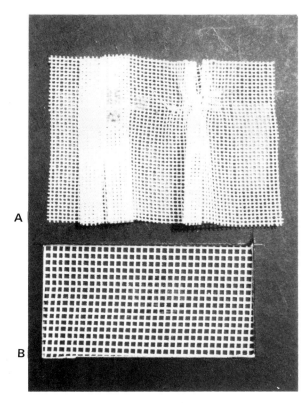

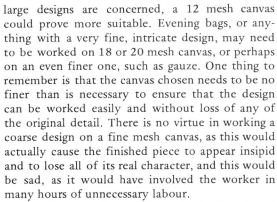

Plastic canvas A 20 threads to 1 in (25 mm)
B 10 threads to 1 in. (25 mm)

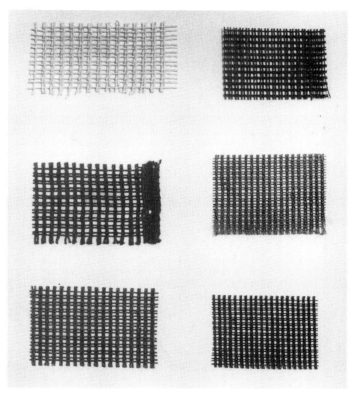

Double-thread (Penelope) Canvas, showing the different meshes available

large designs are concerned, a 12 mesh canvas could prove more suitable. Evening bags, or anything with a very fine, intricate design, may need to be worked on 18 or 20 mesh canvas, or perhaps on an even finer one, such as gauze. One thing to remember is that the canvas chosen needs to be no finer than is necessary to ensure that the design can be worked easily and without loss of any of the original detail. There is no virtue in working a coarse design on a fine mesh canvas, as this would actually cause the finished piece to appear insipid and to lose all of its real character, and this would be sad, as it would have involved the worker in many hours of unnecessary labour.

The best quality canvas obtainable should always be used when working furniture coverings. It can be either single- or double-thread canvas, but single-thread is preferable, as all stitches can be worked on it without difficulty, and it is especially suitable for working tent stitch, the main stitch used in doing this particular type of canvas work, whereas the use of double-thread canvas in working tent stitch often entails separating the double threads, in order to obtain the best effect. Florentine stitch and Rococo stitch can, on the other hand, probably be worked more successfully on double-thread canvas than on single-thread.

For large wall panels and pictures canvas of any quality can be used, and for experimental pieces of work hessian is a possible alternative to canvas. Some experimental work is also occasionally done today on coarse chicken wire instead of canvas, and this practice goes back to the use of fine wire-mesh 'canvas' in the latter years of the nineteenth century for working small, hand-held fire screens. A limp flex canvas, which has replaced the Winchester canvas of Louisa Pesel's day, is still obtainable, but it is a coarser material than the original. Plastic canvas, a new-comer to the canvas-work world, is only available in small pieces, but, as it is a non-fraying material, which is pliable and, at the same time, rigid enough to stand without support, it can be exceedingly useful for three-dimensional work, such as the making of covers for boxes.

One of the best canvases is a natural-coloured,

209

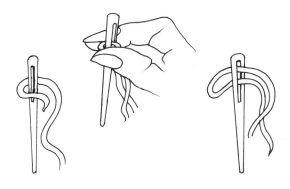

Sketch showing the threading of a needle with wool

polished cotton-thread canvas, which is made in widths of 27 in and 37 in. (69 cm and 91 cm). Cheaper cotton canvases in buff and white are stocked by some large stores, but these, unlike the more expensive ones, have been stiffened by the use of size, and they become sticky, limp and stained, if they come into contact with moisture.

Yarns

The principal yarn used in working canvas-work covers for furniture, and for such things as cushions, handbags or kneelers, as well as for making rugs, is undoubtedly wool or a combination of wool with a little silk. Wool is easy to work with, is strong and covers the threads of the canvas well. Appleton's crewel wool, which is a two-ply wool, made in 382 shades of colour, is hard-wearing and one of the best types of wool to use for furniture coverings. Two strands of this wool are, however, required in the needle, if it is used on a 16 mesh canvas, and for a 14 mesh canvas three strands would be required. Appleton's tapestry wool, which is four-ply, but which can be split if necessary, is suitable for any canvas coarser than 14 mesh. Both types of Appleton's wool are made in the same range of colours and blend well with other wools, such as Medici, Paternayan Persian, Floralia, crepe and knitting wools. They also go well with silks and stranded cottons, Coton Perlé, nylon and the numerous synthetic lurex threads. These latter threads are most useful for working decorative panels and for smaller articles, such as lamp-bases, mirror surrounds, clock faces and numerous other small objects. Any kind of yarn can, in fact, be used for canvas work, provided that it is capable of being pulled easily through the holes in the canvas without causing damage.

Needles and scissors

The needles necessary for working on canvas are known as tapestry needles and are provided with large eyes to take the wool easily and with blunt points to slip through the holes in the canvas without danger of splitting the canvas threads. These needles are easy to thread with the wool, if the worker wraps a length of this yarn around the eye of the needle, pinches it closely together between thumb and fore-finger, slips it gently off the top of the needle and, while still pressing it firmly together, pushes the folded wool through the eye of the needle. (See diagram l). Needles vary in size from a fine 26 to a coarse 13. A number 18 is best for use on a 16 mesh canvas and a number 20 to 22 for anything finer. The eye of a needle, which is to be used for this work, should be just large enough to accommodate the thickness of the yarn being used and it must pass easily through the holes in the canvas without distorting the canvas-threads in any way.

A small, fine pair of scissors is also necessary for this work.

Embroidery frames

Many types of embroidery frame are obtainable, but those best suited for use in canvas work must be strong enough to take the strain of the stretched canvas, which should be kept as tight as a drum. The two types of frame most commonly employed in this work are the flat bar type with split pins or pegs and the screw bar type: the flat-bar frame is the most suitable, particularly when a large piece of canvas has to be worked, as it remains quite rigid under strain, and the canvas can be rolled up when required, in order to leave an area for working which is smaller than can be obtained with the screw bar frame. Another characteristic of the screw bar frame, which makes it less suitable for this work, is the fact that it tends to twist and refuse to lie flat, when the canvas is pulled taut. Simple rectangular frames can easily be made at home from a 2½ in. x 1¾ in (63 mm x 19 mm) batten, which can be cut to the size required and nailed together at the corners. The canvas can be stretched on this type of frame by fixing it to the edge with drawing pins (thumb tacks) or tin tacks or by stapling, but it cannot, of course, be rolled up, as it can on the flat bar frame, mentioned above.

There are other kinds of frame available, such as the floor version of the screw-bar frame, and there is also one small frame, which is sold as a 'travelling' frame, but this latter one is most unsuitable for canvas work, as it is not capable of

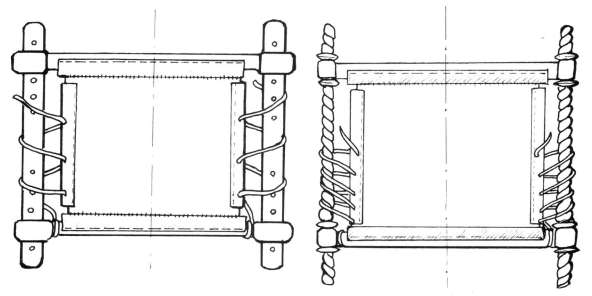

Sketch of flat-bar embroidery frame

Sketch of screw-bar embroidery frame

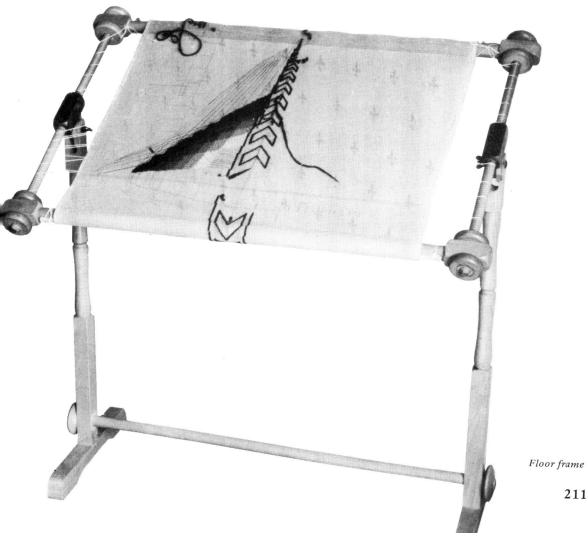

Floor frame

211

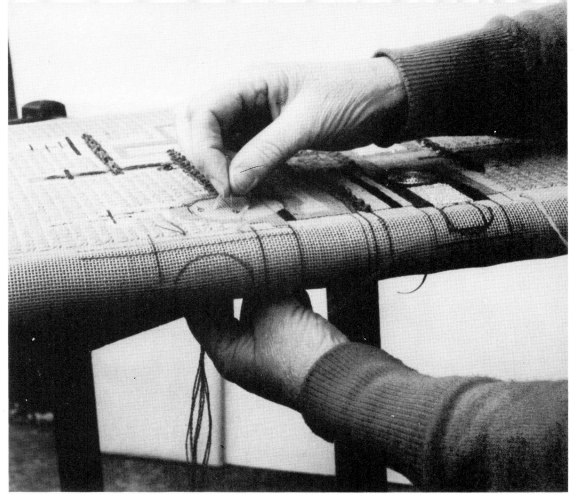

holding the canvas taut. The circular ring frame (tambour frame) is also one which is not suitable for this work, as canvas is a much too heavy material to be used on it.

The flat-bar and screw-bar types of embroidery frames are made with 24 in., 27 in. or 36 in. (61 cm, 69 cm or 91 cm) long tapes attached, so that they will accommodate those widths of canvas, and it is necessary, when buying a frame to specify the length of tape required. Small pieces of canvas do not need to be attached to a frame, as they can be successfully worked in the hand without the danger of their being pulled out of shape in the process. Large pieces should, however, always be worked on a frame, not only because this ensures that the canvas remains taut, but also as it facilitates the working by enabling the embroiderer to have both hands free, one to be kept above the canvas to put the needle into position, and the other below the surface to pull the needle through and find the next hole into which it must go to continue the work further. (See illustration).

Method of working on canvas When the canvas is attached to a frame, both hands can be used in working: one should be kept on the surface of the work, whilst the other is placed under the frame to direct the needle up through the hole in the canvas

Method of working

Transferring designs to canvas

When a design has been drawn on paper, it is then outlined in black, using either a felt-tipped pen or a brush and water-colour paint. The vertical and horizontal centre lines are drawn in in pencil upon the design, and the point of intersection of these lines is marked clearly with a small cross in black in the centre of the design. The four points, where the centre lines meet the outside edges of the design, should also be marked in in black.

The piece of canvas, on to which the design is to be traced, should be two inches larger all round than the design itself and should also have its

Tracing the design on to canvas This picture shows the design pinned in position under the canvas with the centre lines marked in and the tracing just started with black paint

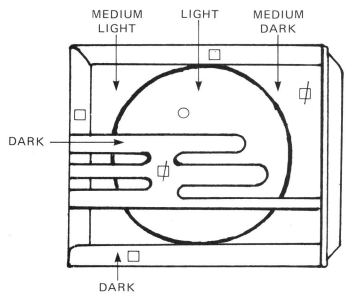

MEDIUM LIGHT   LIGHT   MEDIUM DARK

DARK

DARK

SUGGESTIONS FOR WORKING
☐ PAD AND COVER WITH LEATHER OR VELVET
○ STITCHERY TEXTURED
⧄ STITCHERY FLAT

Method of stitching canvas to the webbing

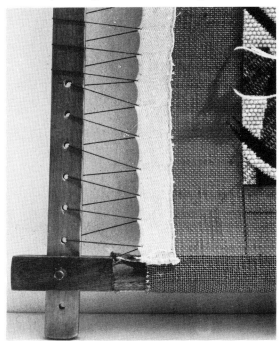

Canvas laced to a flat-bar frame

vertical and horizontal centre lines drawn in in pencil right across the surface. Place the design on a drawing board and pin the canvas into position over it with drawing pins (thumb tacks), so that the centre lines on the canvas exactly match those of the design. This is best done by first putting a drawing-pin directly into the centre of the work, using the black cross in the centre of the design as a guide, and then spreading the canvas out from the centre and pinning it down, so that the points where the centre lines meet the outer edges of the canvas match these same points on the design. It may be necessary to pull the canvas to get it into the correct position, before finally pinning it down all round. The outline of the design should now be clearly visible through the canvas, and tracing can begin.

Trace the design by using a number 5 sable brush and black water-colour paint, mixed on the dry side. A felt-tipped pen can also be used for tracing, but the line made by such a pen can rub off and mark light-coloured silk or wool, unless the pen used is waterproof.

The design can be traced on to the canvas after it has been attached to the embroidery frame, and some workers may prefer this method. The paper design is pinned into position underneath the canvas, and the frame may be moved around in order to get it into a position where the lines of the design are clearly visible for tracing.

Fixing the canvas to the frame

Before the canvas is attached to the frame, four threads along the edge should be turned under and the pencilled centre line matched exactly to the centre line on one of the tapes or strips of webbing already fixed to the rollers of the frame. Starting

214

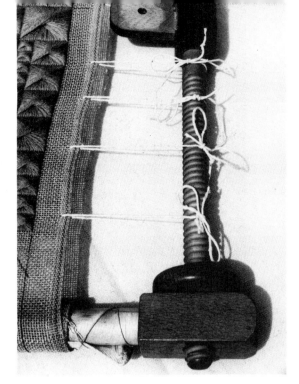

One method of tying the sides of the canvas to a screw-bar frame

canvas by winding it off one roller and on to the other, the webbing must be removed from the edges and then re-attached, when the new area of canvas to be worked has been exposed.

Starting to work

The needle should be threaded with a length of the yarn to be used, measuring approximately 24 in. (60 cm). Anything longer than this is liable to fray and wear thin, as a result of being continually pulled through the canvas. It is a good idea,

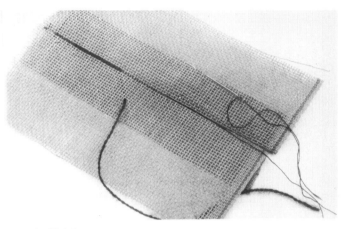

Method of joining canvas

from the centre point and pulling both canvas and webbing taut, oversew the two edges with strong sewing cotton, working outwards from the centre, first to one edge of the canvas and then to the other, and fastenting off the thread securely at both ends. Attach the opposite edge of the piece of canvas to the other roller in the same manner.

The canvas can now be rolled up to a convenient size, and the side struts of the frame put into position through the slots at each end of the rollers and fixed by means of the split pins. One roller should be fixed first, and then the canvas can be stretched to its fullest extent before the other roller is put into position. The canvas should be quite tight before work is begun, and to help achieve this, a piece of webbing should be sewn securely down each side of the canvas and laced to the side-struts of the frame by means of a packing needle and fine, strong twine, which should pass over the side-struts at intervals of about one inch and be fastened off securely at the end. The pieces of webbing thus used must only be as long as the sides of the area of canvas exposed for working, and must not be wound around the rollers, as this would cause a tightening-up of the edges of the canvas, whilst the centre remained slack. When it becomes necessary to move the

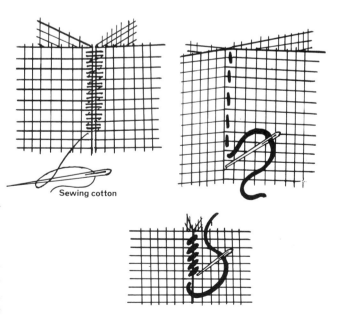

215

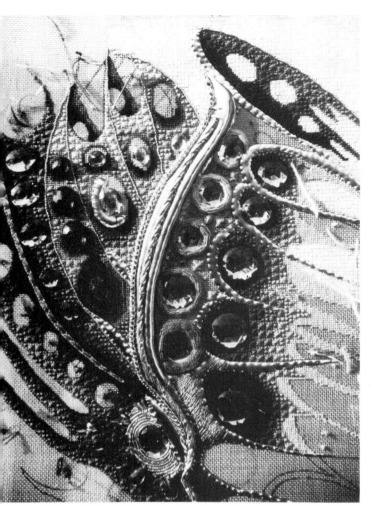

A panel in the process of being worked, early 1970s
This illustration shows clearly the knots and ends of the
working threads, which have been left upon the surface.
The work is being done with silk and wools in shades
of golden yellow, and gold leather, cords and topaz and
amethyst jewels have been applied against a background
of fine, mosaic stitch

before a length of wool is actually used, to pull
it between the first finger and thumb nail, in order
to remove all surplus fluff, which may otherwise clog the holes in the canvas and help to
cause the yarn to wear thin and break.

A knot should be made at the end of the piece
of working yarn, and the needle should be taken
down through the canvas to the underside a short
distance away from the point where the work is

to start, leaving the knot on the surface. When the
length of yarn is finished, the end is again brought
up to the surface of the canvas a short distance
away from the last stitch worked. The knots and
ends of the yarn are left on the surface while the
work continues, until the short lengths of it, which
are left under the canvas, have been made secure
by the working of other stitches, when the knots
and ends on the surface can be cut off. This is the
traditional way of working on canvas, and it keeps
the back of the work completely free of obstruction
from loose ends of yearn, and thus facilitates the
process of working.

When starting a new piece of canvas work, the
design should be worked first, and not the background, as there is always a tendency to encroach
somewhat on to threads of the canvas, which
surround the area being worked. Even when one
does proceed correctly, and works the design first,
it is still possible to lose the true outline of a
shape, especially when square stitches are being
used to fill an area bounded by curves. The best
way to proceed in this case is to outline the
curves carefully with tent stitch before the rest
of the shape is worked, and thus prevent the
awkward stepped effect, which can occur, when
square stitches are used.

Mounting finished work

When a piece of canvas work is finished and taken
off the frame, it will generally need pulling back
into shape. This is particularly the case with pieces
of work in which tent stitch and other diagonal
stitches have been extensively used, as these
stitches tend to pull the canvas out of shape much
more than do square stitches. To stretch the work
it should be placed right side down on a drawing
board, which has first been covered with white
paper or with white cotton material. Avoid using a
sheet of brown paper for this purpose, as it may
stain the work, if water has to be used to aid the
process of stretching. Carefully mark the outline
of the work upon the white paper or cloth
background material, and then stretch the canvas
to fit this shape by first fixing one side of the
work firmly into position with drawing pins
(thumb tacks) placed at intervals of ½ in. (12 mm)
to 1 in. (25 mm) in the surplus threads of canvas
along the edge, and not in the worked part itself,
and then stretching the canvas taut until it reaches
its correct length and can be fixed down with
further drawing pins along the second side. The
canvas can now be stretched to its full width, any
puckers can be smoothed out and the tacks inserted

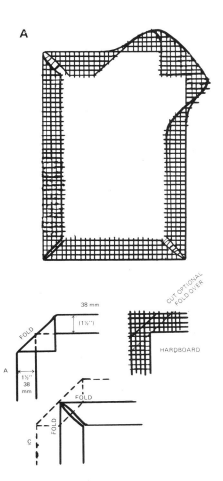

along the remaining edges to hold the work down firmly to the marked shape. If this proves difficult to do, it may be necessary to sprinkle the back of the canvas with water, which should help the process of easing the piece into the required position. It should then be left pinned down for 24 hours to dry, after which it can be carefully removed from the drawing-board and should have returned to its correct shape. The use of water should be avoided on areas of silk, as water penetrates silk more readily than wool or cotton and can cause the surface of the work to become stained. A canvas, which has been stiffened with size, may also become limp and sticky, if it is soaked with water, so only a very limited amount of water should be used, when stretching work done on this type of canvas.

After being stretched, pictures and wall panels in canvas work can be mounted upon hard board, either by glueing them on with a strong adhesive, or by the method of lacing them across the back of the mounting board with fine twine, as shown in the illustration. If, however, the canvas-work panel is large and heavy, it may be necessary to mount it on a strong wooden frame. The canvas is stretched over the frame and fixed all round the outer edge of the frame with 3/8 in. (9 mm) tin tacks, placed at intervals of half an inch. A pair of upholsterer's stretchers may be needed to stretch the last two sides of the canvas into position.

When a chair seat or stool top is to be upholstered with canvas work by a professional, the stretching of the canvas can safelty be left to him.

Framing

Canvas work panels are much improved, if they are framed with a mount covered in linen of a suitable colour placed around them. This has the effect of isolating the embroidery from its immediate surroundings, thus giving it more importance and enhancing its appearance. An important point to remember is that all canvas work should be framed without glass, if it is to be seen to the best advantage, and non-reflective glass should be avoided at all costs, as it has the effect of flattening out the appearance of the beautiful texture of the stitches, which one has spent so many hours trying to attain. Finally, it should also be remembered that heavily textured pieces of work are improved in appearance, when framed, if they are hung upon a wall in a position where the main source of light is from one side of the frame, so that the lumpy stitches will cast a slight shadow and thus add greatly to the textural effect.

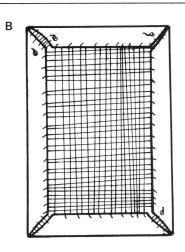

Sketch showing the method of mounting a canvas-work panel A by gluing it on to hardboard B By lacing it on to thick card or hardboard with strong thread

Three-dimensional work

There are various ways in which three-dimensional effects can be achieved in canvas work, and the following are some of them. Worked canvas shapes can be mounted on thick card, or they can be soft-padded, and then attached either to a background of canvas or to any other suitable fabric. This is sometimes done with related shapes, which are then placed together to form a larger shape. String of varying thickness can be sewn on to the canvas and wrapped with silk or wool, or plaited or coiled, or it can simply be looped and attached, as in diagram (k). Canvas can be folded into strips and plaited, and interesting effects can also be obtained, when working with the more flexible types of canvas, if they are simply gathered. Holes can be cut in the canvas to show a lower layer of something contrasting, such as an intricate piece of work on a finer mesh canvas. Wire shapes, depicting such things as leaves and flowers, can be covered with canvas and worked in various stitches, before being stitched into position on the background of such a piece as a canvas-work landscape. Human figures, animals and buildings, worked on separate pieces of canvas, can also be applied to such a piece, being fixed with Velcro to enable them to be moved around on the surface of the landscape at will. Found objects, such as attractive pieces of stone or shells from the beach, can also be used in canvas work to create three-dimensional effects, if they are glued or sewn to the surface of the work, and they can be associated in such work with beads, buttons and jewels, and even with such objects as pieces of tree bark. The surface of a canvas-work panel can be enlivened by attaching to it pieces of card, covered with gold leather or velvet, or with some other fabric, such as tweed, or by using beautiful ribbons, both wide and narrow, which mix exceedingly well with canvas-work stitches.

Three dimensional objects

Table lamp bases

Attractive table lamp bases can be made by working a rectangular shape on canvas, which is then wrapped around and securely attached to a suitable piece of tubing of some kind. Plastic piping, such as is used by builders for boiler chimneys, or cardboard tubing, on which carpets are rolled, is quite good for this purpose. It is necessary to obtain a suitably-sized piece before beginning to work the covering, so that the

Design for a three-dimensional panel, using couched string and stitchery on a coarse canvas

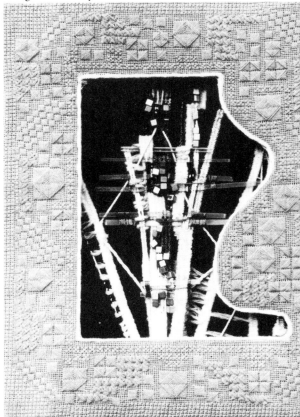

Three-dimensional panel An inner panel of woven threads and wooden beads is enclosed by a canvas-work surround, which has been worked with a variety of stitches

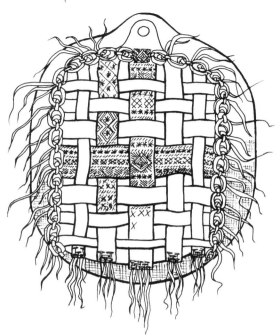

Sketch for a three-dimensional wall-hanging A large hole has been cut in the canvas and strips of plaited canvas of varying width, worked in suitable stitches, have been inserted. The diagram shows double knot stitch used to outline the plaited area, and Turkey rug knot could be used for working the straggly fringe. A whole variety of stitches could be used for working the plaited strips

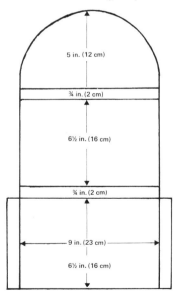

5 in. (12 cm)

¾ in. (2 cm)

6½ in. (16 cm)

¾ in. (2 cm)

9 in. (23 cm)

6½ in. (16 cm)

Clutch bag 9 in. x 6½ in. (23 cm x 16 cm) with ¾ in. (2 cm) gusset
Cut out and worked in one piece makes this the cheapest of all bags to make. It can be fastened with a zip or with one or two press-studs

dimensions of the work can be calculated, before the design is drawn up.

Small three-dimensional objects

Numerous objects can be worked on canvas, which are small enough to be worked in the hand, thus dispensing with the usual embroidery frame. Among these are such articles as belts, collars, costume jewellery, day and evening handbags, purses, powder compacts, pin cushions, bell pulls, paper weights, finger plates, boxes, small cushions, book covers, desk blotters and containers for pens and pencils or for dried flowers. Large pebbles, gathered from the garden or beach, make ideal paper weights, when they have been covered with canvas work. Finger plates, which incorporate small pieces of embroidery, worked in silk on a fine-mesh canvas of 20 threads to the inch, can look very attractive when mounted. They have to be covered with glass or perspex to protect the embroidery.

When working evening bags which require a metal frame, it is advisable to obtain the frame first, before deciding on the shape and size of the bag. Day-time handbags are naturally not so ornamental as evening bags, but nevertheless they can still be gay and glamorous. They can be either the kind of bag which requires a handle, or the flap-over type of bag, which is the easiest of all to make, having the back, the front, the flap-over panel and the gussets all worked in one piece (See diagram).

To make collars, cuffs, belts or costume ornaments, the outline of the required shape is marked on the canvas and then cut out, leaving a margin of canvas approximately ¾ in. (2 cm) wide all round. For costume ornaments small metal shapes may be obtained in certain craft shops, which are intended for enamelling purposes, and these are ideal for mounting canvas work and being used as pendants. If a particular shape of pendant is needed, a section of a tin can may be cut to the shape which is required by using an old pair of kitchen scissors. Card can be used as a base for such work, but a metal base is better, as it gives just sufficient weight for a pendant to hang well.

Boxes of various shapes, when covered with canvas work and beautifully lined and finished off, make lovely and very acceptable presents. An existing tin or cardboard box can prove quite suitable for covering in this way, or, if necessary, a box can be made from stout card to the measurements required, and a thinner card, covered with lining material, can be inserted inside it.

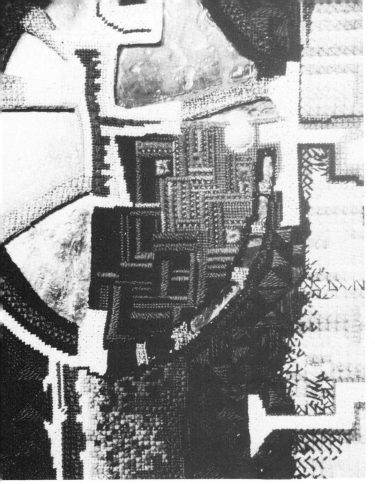

Small three-dimensional picture, worked on 16-mesh canvas by Jean Shilton, 1981   The foreground and the sky are worked in straight stitches with coarse wool, and the trees are worked with couched boucle wool. The white cottage has been worked separately and stands away from the background. *Velcro* has been attached to the back of the cottage, so that it can be removed and and then replaced

Detail of a panel, showing sections of the canvas cut out to reveal an area of stained glass

This very free method of working was ideal for the purpose of advertising, and this particular piece appeared in colour as a double-page spread in several national magazines and was used for a poster to advertise Jaeger hand-knitting yarns in the winter of 1978 *Barbara Siedlecka*

Skanes, designed and worked by the author, 1970s. This panel was based on groups of stones found on a beach. These were stitched on to the canvas, and the design was then developed around them by using woollen yarns and string

Design for a canvas-work clock-face and surround

Small three-dimensional panel   A modern design worked on 16-mesh canvas mainly in tent stitch, using silk, cotton, lurex thread, wool, raffia and string. The colours are silver, black, white and shades of blue

Reflections, designed and worked by Jean Colgan, 1980. This canvas-work panel shows a freely-worked landscape scene. The heavy rock formation on the right-hand side is highly padded and covered with black leather

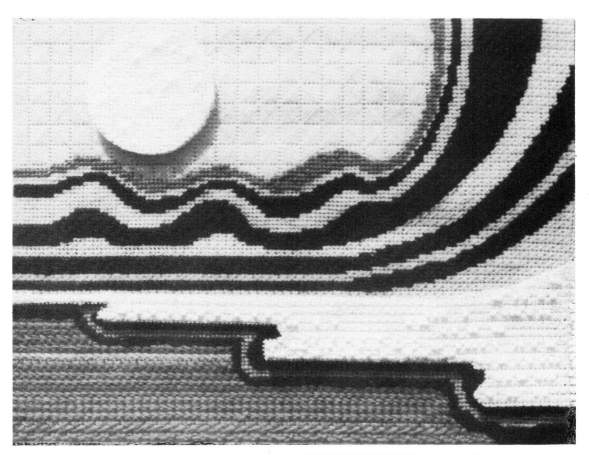

Winter Seascape, designed and worked by the author,
1980   A three-dimensional panel, worked on plastic
canvas

Lamp base, worked by Winnie Browning, 1970s   The
cover for the lamp base is worked on 16-mesh canvas
with wool and rayon. It is mounted upon a tube like
the one shown with its ply-wood top and bottom in
position. The centre line for indicating where the canvas
cover will be fixed is also shown, and there is a hole for
inserting the flex

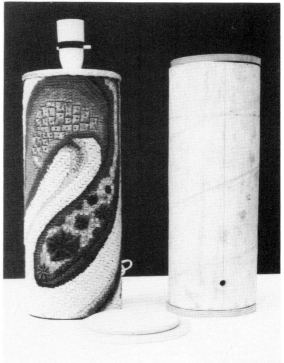

Free-standing flower shapes, worked by Olive Castelton, 1970s   Wired canvas has been worked in a variety of stitches

Sketches for three-dimensional canvas-work designs

225

Three-dimensional wall-hanging by Valerie Harding

Three-dimensional canvas-work panel, worked by Doris
Warans, 1976   This panel was worked with cotton, wool
and metallic thread in a wide variety of stitches

Mirror-surround by Valerie Harding

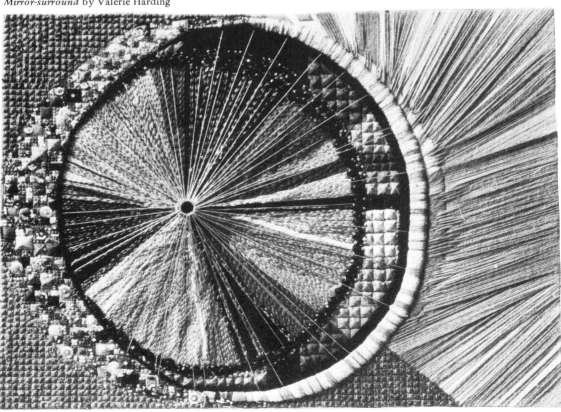

Detail of a Turkey-work panel, designed and worked by Patricia Trott, 1971   This piece was worked on 14-mesh single canvas in Ghiordes knot stitch (Turkey rug-knot) with polychrome wool

Evening bag, worked by Rose Cussens, 1960s   The background of this attractive evening bag is worked in cushion stitch with twisted embroidery silk. Gold leather and couched gold thread have also been used in working the design, together with jewels

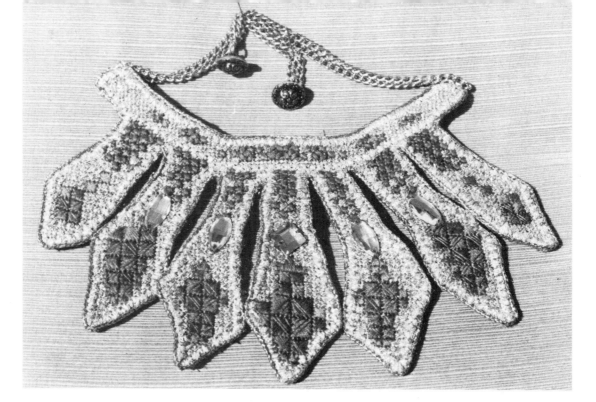

Neckpiece, designed and worked by the author, 1974
This piece is worked on 18-mesh canvas with silk, fine
wool and Twilley's gold-fingering in mosaic, Smyrna and
cross-cornered cushion stitches, and has some jewels
applied

Pendant, designed and worked by the author, 1970s
Blue and green silk and silver thread have been used with
pearls in making this canvas-work pendant

Mirror-surround, worked by Doris Cloake, 1973   A ▷
finished canvas for a mirror-surround before mounting

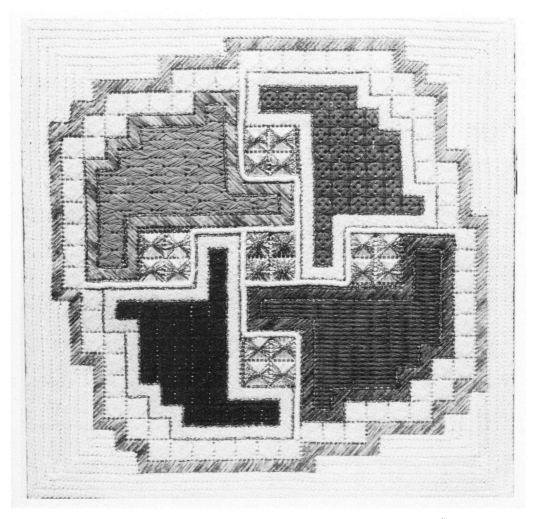

Stone Garden, designed and worked by the author, 1970s. A panel worked on double-thread, coarse canvas with four threads to the inch (25 mm)

Coffee-table-top, worked by Rösli Warren, early 1970s This is a tent-stitch design on a background of cushion stitch. It is worked on 16-mesh, single-thread canvas with silk and wool

Amoeba Panel, worked by Lilian Hill, early 1970s   This panel is worked on 16-mesh canvas in tent and Smyrna stitches, used together with a few beads and some laid string, and with isolated wheatsheaf stitches worked over an area of tent stitch to form an attractive background

Robert Burns' Cottage in Ayr, Scotland, worked by Anna Bowden, 1975   An interesting small picture of a famous cottage, worked on 16-mesh canvas with wool and silk in some well-chosen stitches

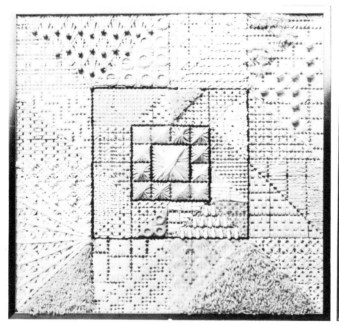

Squares and Triangles, worked by Jean Shilton, 1975
This panel is worked on rug-canvas with four double-threads to one inch. It is attractively worked in a variety of stitches, using yarn in shades of cream and white. Beads and covered curtain rings have also been used. The centre panel is outlined with brown wool in back stitch

God and Man, designed and worked by Jean Shilton for the Spiritualist Church at Eltham, London, 1976   Circles, broken by a number of triangular shapes, radiate from a central jewel. The design is in gold, silver and shades of blue

Rock Candy, worked by Doris Cloake, 1977   A small, bright and lively panel, worked in clear pinks, orange and red, outlined with goldfingering on a white and gold background. The diagonal cross is worked in jewel shades of ruby red, blue and green with gold. The corners are left unworked, as the piece was to be mounted on an inch-thick (25 mm) board

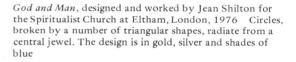

Japanese Ladies, worked by Miriam Bawden, 1978   ▷
Horizontal fishbone stitch has been successfully used for working the sky, which is in silk, and the tiny zigzag back stitch has been used with equal success for the foreground. The ladies' skirts are resplendent in a mixture of fine wool and metal thread, the one on the left being worked in four-part-eye stitch, while the other is worked in fine rice stitch over two threads of the canvas

233

The Mill Stream, worked by Doris Cloake, 1979   The impression gained by looking at this canvas-work picture with its varied use of stitches is that it is unmistakenly an embroidery and not a painting

Cushion cover, designed and worked by the author, 1981 Ribbon has been applied to the canvas, and various stitches such as Rhodes, Smyrna, rice and long-legged cross stitch have been worked as a background to make an attractive small cushion

Fighting Cocks, worked by Nellie J Old, 1982   This
circular panel, which is based on a Chinese design, is
worked on 16-mesh single canvas in tent and satin stitches.
Close-cover stitch is used for working the background,
while Rhodes stitch in goldfingering surrounds the circle

Canvas work is by its very nature a luxury craft,
requiring a great deal of time and careful application to bring it to completion, so thought should
be given to the desirability of using it in covering
such a mundane thing as a brick, in order to make
a doorstop!

Further reading

The Livery Companies of the City of London, W C Hazlitt, 1837
Royal Bookbindings, Cyril Davenport, Seely & Co Ltd, 1896
Samplers, Leigh Ashton, Medici Society, 1926
English Embroidery, Vols I and II, Cross Stitch, Luisa Pesel, Batsford, 1931
American Needlework, Georgiana Brown Harbeson, Bonanza Books, 1938
English Historical Embroidery, Barbara Snook, Batsford, 1960
The Irwin Untermyer Collection, text by Yvonne Hackenbroch, Thames and Hudson, 1960
Victorian Embroidery, Barbara Morris, Hubert Jenkins, 1962
English Mediaeval Carpets, 16th — 19th Century, M J Mayorcas, F Lewis, 1963
William Morris, Philip Henderson, Thames & Hudson, 1965
A History of British Carpets, C E G Tattersall and S Reed, 1966
History of Western Embroidery, Mary Eirwen Jones, Studio Vista, 1969
Victorian Canvas Work, Molly Proctor, Batsford, 1972
Samplers, Anne Sebba, Weidenfeld and Nicolson, 1979
Figures in Fabric, Margaret Swain, Barry & Jenkins

Index